"I Do"

To order additional copies of *I Do*, by Gábor Mihalec,
call 1-800-765-6955.

Visit us at **www.reviewandherald.com** for information
on other Review and Herald® products.

"I Do"

{How to build a *great* marriage}

Gábor Mihalec, Ph.D.

REVIEW AND HERALD® PUBLISHING ASSOCIATION
Since 1861 | www.reviewandherald.com

Copyright © 2014 by Review and Herald® Publishing Association

Published by Review and Herald® Publishing Association, Hagerstown, MD 21741-1119

All rights reserved. No portion of this book may be reproduced, stored in a retrieval system, or transmitted in any form or by any means (electronic, mechanical, photocopy, recording, scanning, or other), except for brief quotations in critical reviews or articles, without the prior written permission of the publisher.

Review and Herald® titles may be purchased in bulk for educational, business, fund-raising, or sales promotional use. For information, e-mail SpecialMarkets@reviewandherald.com.

The Review and Herald® Publishing Association publishes biblically based materials for spiritual, physical, and mental growth and Christian discipleship.

Texts credited to NIV are from the *Holy Bible, New International Version.* Copyright © 1973, 1978, 1984, 2011 by Biblica, Inc. Used by permission. All rights reserved worldwide.

Texts credited to NKJV are from the New King James Version. Copyright © 1979, 1980, 1982 by Thomas Nelson, Inc. Used by permission. All rights reserved.

This book was
Edited by Amy Prindle and Gerald Wheeler
Copyedited by Delma Miller
Designed by Emily Ford / Review and Herald® Design Center
Cover art by Thinkstock.com
Typeset: 12.5/15 Minion Pro

PRINTED IN U.S.A.

18 17 16 15 14   5 4 3 2 1

Library of Congress Cataloging-in-Publication Data
Mihalec, Gabor, 1974-   .
  I do : how to build a great marriage / Gabor Mihalec.
     pages cm
  Includes bibliographical references.
  ISBN 978-0-8280-2749-6
  1. Marriage counseling. 2. Marriage. 3. Marriage--Religious aspects--Christianity. I. Title.
  HQ10.M545 2014
  306.81--dc23
                              2013015347

ISBN 978-0-8280-2749-6

{ **to dora:** *my companion, friend, and love* }

{ contents: }

Foreword		9
Preface:	Dear Couple	11
Chapter 1:	Preparing for Marriage: How Can I Know if I've Found "The One"?	15
Chapter 2:	It's Time to Think Again	20
Chapter 3:	Spouse, Domestic Partner, or POSSLQ?	23
Chapter 4:	Marriage Preparation: Why, How, With Whom, and for How Much?	33
Chapter 5:	The Goal of Marriage: 1+1=1	38
Chapter 6:	Communication: The Art of Listening	45
Chapter 7:	Conflict Resolution: Stumbling Blocks or Stepping-stones	60
Chapter 8:	Personality: Mr. and Mrs. Mystery	73
Chapter 9:	Finances: Gross Dreams and Net Income	83
Chapter 10:	Sexuality: Emotion in Motion	92
Chapter 11:	Parenting: The Making of Mom and Dad	100
Chapter 12:	Leisure Activities: Switching Off the Routine	109
Chapter 13:	Relations: Taming Your In-laws	114
Chapter 14:	Roles and Relationships: Housekeeping in Style	122
Chapter 15:	Spirituality: Moving Mountains	128
Chapter 16:	Boundaries: Mind the Gap!	135
Chapter 17:	Special Issues in Preparation for Marriage	143
Chapter 18:	Life Stages of Marriage	149
Chapter 19:	Mandatory Service for Married Couples	159
Appendix		163
Notes		172

{ foreword: }

Weddings are a time for great celebration. Parents (usually mothers) and their daughters often plan for a long time to have a grand fairy-tale affair. We have been amazed, as we have worked for many years with couples preparing for marriage, how much money they will spend to have an unforgettable wedding day.

While having a lavish wedding ceremony with smartly attired attendants, a well-decorated church or hall, and many guests is certainly important, far more significant is being well prepared for marriage.

Marriage instability and dissatisfaction are major concerns the world over, despite well-established and instituted cultural norms in certain societies to avoid the dissolution of many fragile unions.

In this important labor of love our colleague and friend Gábor Mihalec, from Hungary, offers couples who are serious about preparing well for the most crucial enterprise in their lives a road map to marital stability and satisfaction.

Mihalec understands his craft well and offers to trained pastors and other clinicians evidence-based tools and relational skills that when taught well to premarital couples will result in a higher probability of stronger and healthier marriages.

We wish you God's blessings, whether you are planning on getting married in the near future or are about to guide a couple preparing for marriage. Regardless, this volume will serve you well as you engage in the process of building a great marriage.

— **Willie and Elaine Oliver, Directors**
Department of Family Ministries
General Conference of Seventh-day Adventists
Silver Spring, Maryland

{ preface: }
dear couple

You are surely living one of the most beautiful, exciting, and eventful periods of your life. The great day is getting closer and closer. But you still have quite a few nagging entries on your to-do list that you haven't been able to sort out yet. And during the process of organizing, you have most likely discovered that you two do not think as similarly as you may have before . . .

Are you sure you thought of everything? Nothing of major importance was forgotten?

Have you already found the perfect location worthy of the happiest event of your life so far? Have you agreed upon a wedding planner? Have you made your choice concerning a pastor or wedding official? Do you have the dress, the suit, and all the small but important accessories? And what about the honeymoon? Is it already organized so that everything can go smoothly on your first trip as a married couple? (Believe me, you will desperately need a good rest after the wedding!)

If you have all to-do's checked, then there is only one thing to prepare for: *the marriage!* All the things listed previously concern only one day of your life: the wedding day. But marriage is not for only a day. Marriage (and I wholeheartedly wish you a happy one)—will be all the days *after* your wedding day. I assume that if you are preparing extensively for this big day, you will prepare for your marriage even more.

I'd like to contribute to your preparation with this handbook. Because I know very well that during this busy time of your life you don't have many chances to read, I have tried to focus on the most important elements of a marriage. As a result I wrote every chapter in such a manner that you can read any of them independently.

I trust that my relaxed approach on the subject will be bearable even for a typical man, despite the fact that there will be no technical equipment involved—only relational stuff. And once you are back from your honeymoon, you can pick up this book, read it again, and discuss the chapters in sequence. Also, for an easier reading experience, I have listed the references and resources in comprehensive endnotes. Additionally, I hope you will find the exercises at the end of each chapter helpful. I encourage you to do them all, as the real benefit of this book is not in the knowledge you will gain but in the understanding of your relationship that will become reality as you work together.

Of course, the material published in this book is not only useful for dating or engaged couples; it can also be of help for those who have been together for a long time or are already married and would like to see their life from a new angle. For them, this joint adventure can be the first step of a fresh start.

This book is the product of 17 years of marriage, as well as many hours of couple counseling and therapy with premarital and married couples. But there is still more. As a marriage counselor I have always considered it important to keep my work from being guided solely by personal observations and experience, and instead to base it on the results of sound, scientific research. Three leading scholars of this field have especially influenced my knowledge about marriage and marriage preparation:

David H. Olson has been continuously publishing epoch-making research in marriage education and counseling since 1968. The most important fruit of his work is the PREPARE/ENRICH relationship program. More than 3 million couples have completed its inventories. As a result, LIFE INNOVATIONS, Inc.—also founded by him—owns the largest database of couples' relationship data. It was a special honor that, together with my friend and colleague Robert Csizmadia, I could translate Olson's relationship inventories into Hungarian and train approximately 200 facilitators to use the system.

John M. Gottman became world-famous by his "Love Laboratory" in Seattle,

Washington. The Love Laboratory is a very comfortable apartment with cameras and microphones in every room (except the bedroom and bathroom) that record the conversations of the couples that move into it for a few days. What's more, the residents wear various devices on their bodies that monitor their blood pressure, pulse rates, and other physiological signals. Thousands of couples have temporarily lived in it for the past three decades, and Gottman has used their data to establish a therapeutic system that can provide a very accurate prognosis of a relationship's future.

Gottman said in a recent interview that it was enough for him to observe a couple for three minutes, and he could not only predict *whether* they would get divorced, but also *when*. And if Gottman says it, I can believe it, because behind every sentence he writes there stand hard figures of scientific analysis.

Andreas Bochmann was my professor for three years during my university studies in Germany. Bochmann has led several research endeavors looking at methods of marriage preparation, sexual relationship satisfaction, divorce and remarriage, and the relation of religion and couple relationship. He is also one of the first European representatives of David Olson's PREPARE/ENRICH program.

I will cite all three of these experts quite frequently, so you can be sure that this book is based on leading scientific research. But I will give advice only on what I have tried myself and found beneficial.

Finally, let me say some words about the extended edition. This book has already debuted in an earlier release. Thanks to a generous donation for the first release, I published a 100-page version of 22,500 copies in Hungary during 2010. They were distributed to registrars across the country and handed to couples preparing for marriage. Thus the first edition of this book became the biggest publication on marriage education in Hungary to date. The book secured the commendation of well-known experts in the field of relationship enrichment and marriage preparation: Emőke Bagdy, Jenő Ranschburg, Mária Pándy, and many others. Several professional and academic organizations included the book in their training materials. I'm very grateful for their encouragement and suggestions.

I wish you joy and exciting discoveries while reading this book.

—Gábor Mihalec

1

{ preparing for marriage: }
how can I know if I've found "the one"?

The disturbing "second thought" before the wedding is the subject of many romantic comedies. Am I sure this person is the right choice for me? Is it a good decision to get married now, and to him or her? I also remember such feelings from my own life. During my engagement, nothing could have made me happier than to receive a warranty card stating that I had chosen well, that Dora would be the best for me, and that we would have a happy, lifelong relationship. But this kind of warranty does not exist. To put it more precisely, such a guarantee does not exist in writing, but it can exist in us. *A happy marriage is the common result of the cooperative efforts of both parties.*

I will keep repeating this fundamental thesis. The guarantee exists in the efforts that the parties put into their relationship. Some compare marriage to a garden. If a person wants his or her garden to look beautiful, give joy, and fill the air with wonderful scents, then that individual needs to work for it. Nothing good will happen by itself. The only thing that grows naturally by itself in a garden is weeds—you don't need to do anything for that to happen. The same is true for a marriage. If we do nothing to cultivate our relationship, it will drift toward disaster. But if we put effort into it, if we keep it in our focus and continually look after it, it will grow into a prosperous, fruitful, and mutually happy relationship. Not because problems never occur, but because the right attitude helps us transform difficulties into advantages. We can learn to turn the stumbling blocks into stepping-stones.[1] This is the second fundamental thesis I will repeat again and again: A stone lying in front of us usually causes us to trip. Many marriages are prone to fail because of the problems that will arise in life. But with conscious efforts, any couple can turn the stumbling blocks into stepping-stones and reach higher in their relationship.

> 28% of couples surveyed in the 1990s had the opportunity of courting the old-fashioned way.

If you will remember from this book only these two theses—"*A happy marriage is the common result of the cooperative efforts of both parties*" and that with conscious efforts "*we can turn stumbling blocks into stepping-stones*"—you will have a "first-aid kit" that can save your relationship during a critical situation. You can, however, learn much more.

Let's examine the first important step toward a happy marriage: the ideal choice of marriage partner. How can you determine, with certainty, the right person with whom you can live happily ever after?

The Characteristics of an Ideal Wife- or Husband-to-be

The ideal husband is 24-30 years old, around six feet tall, about 150-175 pounds, has an athletic body, hasn't started to lose his hair yet, wears fashionable glasses that make him look intellectual, wears a neat, short, trimmed beard, has two master's degrees, drives a family car, and lives on his own property . . .

The ideal wife-to-be is around 22-28 years old, about five and a half feet tall, and 110-140 pounds. She is always kind and happy, slim yet curvy, has silky long hair that sweeps the ground, knows all the secret family recipes by heart, speaks several languages, and says yes to her husband in each of them . . .

Many people have such "ideals" in mind when it comes to choosing a spouse. They believe that there must be a person who can live up to all these expectations, and the only job on their part is to find that individual and make him or her fall in love. But the reality is very different. In actuality, the most important selection criterion is compatibility. It measures how well two individuals can "fit" together. But what are the areas or characteristics in which the two need to be in harmony? What constitutes the core of a relationship?

Several areas of a marriage will especially affect the couple's happiness: realistic expectations, accepting and adapting to each other's personalities, good communication, effective conflict resolution, skilled handling of family finances, balancing leisure time and work time, coordinating activities spent individually or collectively, harmony in sexuality and affection, preparing for parenting and a willingness to fulfill in its tasks, accepting each other's family and friends, agreeing on the roles in the relationship, understanding and living out spirituality, and finding balance in closeness and flexibility (I will explain both concepts later in the book). The more areas that are compatible, the better the chance for a happy, long-lasting, four-star marriage.

Some couples have a compatibility that seems to exist right out of the box, while others have to work at it for several years. It doesn't matter in which group they belong at the beginning of their relationship—what is more important is the couple's ultimate goals and the hard work they put into achieving them. Let's look at the possible outcomes.

The Four-Star Choice

David H. Olson's research has shown that the happiest couples are those who fit together in all of the areas listed above, meaning that they have similar views and opinions in each area. It does not demand that they were born to be alike, but rather that they have had a lot of discussions with each other and have worked out agreements in all (or at least most) areas of the relationship. Each area is then strong. They have a vivid and growing relationship, and according to the official terminology, it is "vitalized." Typically the people around them recognize this; therefore, their parents and friends are very positive about their relationship. Such couples have the greatest statistical chance to be happy and will not separate. Most of them did not live together before the marriage, so they had the opportunity to get to know each other well without any kind of pressure (e.g., living expenses, bills, etc.). They had long talks and planned a common future. In other words, they had the opportunity of courting the old-fashioned way. Unfortunately, fewer and fewer belong to this category. As long ago as the 1990s only 28 percent of couples surveyed fit into this category.[2]

The Three-Star Choice

If we spend the first week of our vacation in a four-star hotel and the next in a three-star one on the other end of the same island, we will not observe many differences—except perhaps the number of TV channels and bottles in the minibar. The same is

> *"A happy marriage is the common result of the cooperative efforts of both parties."*

{preparing for marriage}

true of this group when compared to the one previously examined. The couples with a three-star relationship have as good a time as the four-star couples, though they do score lower in some areas. Generally the weaker areas involve parenting (e.g., they don't yet know or can't agree with each other on how many children they want), realistic expectations (they do not have a true assessment of each other or of their relationship, as though looking through rose-colored glasses that will inevitably break and lead to a painful collision with reality), and spirituality (spirituality doesn't have a role in their lives, they have different spiritual views, or they act on their values in very different ways). However, sooner or later they can compromise and enjoy a balanced, harmonious marriage. Their chance for divorce is slightly greater than that of four-star couples. In the survey mentioned above, 27 percent of the couples fell into this category.

The Two-Star Choice

Continuing the analogy of vacations, we will note significant differences between a four-star and a two-star hotel. In a two-star place one might find that the quality of furniture and facilities is lower, and even the cleanliness might be somewhat suspicious. Similar parallels appear in the two-star relationship. Such couples usually show very good compatibility in areas based on traditional values (parenthood, family and friends, spirituality, traditional relationship roles, etc.), but they fail to perform well in other categories, such as communication, conflict resolution, or being able to accept different personalities. If they cannot talk honestly with each other they cannot solve their differences, and it will have a negative effect on the core of their relationship: intimacy. Surprisingly, such couples rarely get divorced. However, research has shown that the durability of such relationships results from the traditionalist mind-set typical of such couples. Many two-star pairs stay married even if they are unhappy in their relationship. Roughly one quarter (23 percent) of engaged couples belong to this category.

The One-Star Choice

Here a typical comment of the couple's friends is "Find your common sense and think over it again!" The notable feature of these relationships is tension. This kind of couple can make the counselor sweat. It doesn't matter which area of their relationship you look at—they all reveal shortcomings. The couple can argue over anything, no matter the topic. But during a counseling session, when they get to the area of sexuality, a smile grows on their face, and the counselor can rest assured that at least one area is working. But as soon as one examines this area in depth, it becomes clear that even it only *seems* strong, because as long as they are in bed they do not have to talk, resolve conflicts, sort out finances, or deal with in-laws. However, after a few years they will not be sexually attractive to each other, and then it will become obvious that they have nothing that really keeps them together. Therefore, be careful with premarital sex! The development of long-lasting marital strength in relationship dimensions such as communication and conflict resolution is essential, but early sex takes over the relationship's focus and forms an obstacle to the development of such communication. Studies show that many such couples have been living together before the marriage and often find themselves held together only by sex and joint debt (home loan, credit cards, etc.) at the time of the wedding. Because of the very high divorce rate of tense couples, it is vital for them to go through marriage preparation. Twenty-two percent of premarital couples belong to this category.

Summary in Statistics

It is not hard to see that the number of stars in your choice will determine not only the level of happiness but also the future prospect of the relationship. Based on the category in which you belong, one can make a cautious but statistically accurate guess regarding the length of the resulting marriage. Here's how it looks in real numbers:[3]

	Married Satisfied	Married Dissatisfied	Separated or Divorced	Canceled Marriage
Vitalized ****	51%	20%	15%	15%
Harmonious ***	28%	22%	19%	24%
Traditional **	23%	34%	11%	32%
Conflicted *	11%	19%	34%	37%

The chart shows that the vitalized couples have the greatest chance to enjoy a fulfilling, happy marriage. However, only 11 percent of the conflicted (tensed) couples will be happily married. Why is it important to know this? No matter the category in which you belong, it is good to be aware of these figures so as to gain perspective, because with conscious effort you can further develop your relationship and collect more stars! By now you should realize that a happy marriage is the result of the cooperative efforts of both parties. And if at times you fail, remind yourself that you can still turn the stumbling blocks into stepping-stones!

---

[1] David H. Olson, Amy Olson-Sigg, and Peter J. Larson, *The Couple Checkup* (Nashville: Thomas Nelson, 2008), p. 18.

[2] D. H. Olson and B. J. Fowers, "Four Types of Premarital Couples: An Empirical Typology Based on PREPARE," *Journal of Family Psychology* 6 (1992): 10-21.

[3] D. H. Olson, B. J. Fowers, and K. H. Montel, "Predicting Marital Success for Premarital Couple Types Based on PREPARE," *Journal of Marital and Family Therapy* 22 (1996): 103-119.

2

{ it's time to think again }

We looked into the "stars," but let's get back down to earth. In this chapter I will describe issues that should prompt you to reconsider your wedding, as the following situations carry great risk to the durability of marriage.*

1. The pair meets or marries immediately after a severe loss. There will arise situations in which a person gets involved in a relationship not because of a mutual emotional attraction, but because one wants to help the other, who is going through a hard time. For example, two people are friends and one gives emotional aid to the other, who just left a relationship. A relationship based upon such an emotional connection has an inherent instability (though also a special emotional bond), and it easily turns the comforting friend into a partner.

Often, however, the relationship changes when the crisis is successfully resolved—the suffering person, who regained the ability to be independent, once again considers the partner as "only" a friend, but often by this time the "friend" might be wearing a wedding ring.

2. A desire to separate from the family of origin/upbringing plays a role in the marriage plans. A need to escape one's family can be acceptable at times (abuse, alcohol problems, etc.). However, it does not mean that it should happen by way of getting married. In most cases the preferable way for a young adult to gain independence is to move out from the family home and build up his or her own life, taking the opportunity to develop a new relationship with the parents. Otherwise there's a good chance that the person will simply flee from bad to eventually worse.

3. The family background of the parties involved is significantly different (religion, upbringing, values, social status, ethnic roots, age, etc.). They say opposites attract, but such a belief has only limited validity when it comes to marriage. Because it is true that nobody is perfect, married partners can enrich each other's lives with their individual strengths. On the other hand, being alike in ethical values, religious convictions, and other important parts of identity will ultimately be most beneficial. Differences in such major areas can cause serious conflicts, especially during child-rearing.

4. One or both parties are too closely or too loosely linked to their family of origin. Marriage is a community of two individuals with independent identities. If either person is too attached to the parents, the latter tend to feel entitled to meddle in the couple's life. However, if the family of origin is too emotionally distant, a real possibility exists that the grown-up child preparing to get married did not develop the necessary emotional security, affection, or intimacy required for a close relationship. Just as in other areas of life, it is good to avoid extremes in emotional bonding as well. For instance, we all miss our loved one when he or she is not nearby, but we should be able to spend an evening without him or her!

5. The couple is dependent financially, physically, or psychologically on any or both of the families of origin. This point is closely related to the previous one. It is good when parents are able to support the young couple at the start of their marriage. But such aid can easily get abused. Many parents feel that if they give something, it also buys them the right to participate in the decisions of the newlyweds' lives. For this reason I always counsel every premarital couple to keep just enough physical and emotional distance from their parents so that they "cannot come over in slippers."

6. The people to be married are younger than 20 years old. Research shows that the later a person enters into the marriage, the greater the chance it will be lasting and happy. Naturally, it doesn't demand that they have to wait until retirement in order to have a happy marriage. But it does mean that it takes the teenage years (for some, even their early 20s) to form a solid identity. Thus, for an unmatured person to enter into marriage or even a serious relationship without knowing who he or she is or what he or she wants to do is usually a ticking time bomb.

7. The couple dated less than six months or more than three years before getting married. In order to make a reasonable decision concerning marriage, something that will influence the rest of your life, you ought to know the other person pretty well. And it takes time to get to know an individual. If that period is less than half a year, the acquaintance will likely be superficial, and unpleasant surprises might be waiting in the future. However, if the "courtship" lasts longer than three years, it may indicate that the parties are uncertain about each other. Of course, reasonable delays, such as studies, foreign employment, etc., can postpone marriage for a while.

> **Research shows that the later a person enters into the marriage, the greater the chance it will be lasting and happy.**

8. The wedding takes place without the presence of family and friends. Love causes blindness at times. But if even the immediate family members do not participate in the wedding ceremony, it might indicate several things: the newlyweds cannot stand by each other in front of their families, or the family does not agree with their choice and protests their union by staying away. In both cases it is worthwhile to rethink the ceremony and find a solution to the problem.

9. The woman gets pregnant before the wedding or in the first year of marriage. Under no circumstances are forced marriages a good move to make. The fact that the parties have shared the same bed is not an accurate indicator that they would fit together for a full lifetime, supporting each other in both good and bad. Every relationship needs time and the opportunity to develop at its own pace. This is why most professionals look at early pregnancy with reservations. The couple has to establish their own life with its specific rules and frameworks, and it is easier for everyone when no third parties are present, even "just" a baby.

10. One or both parties declare that they had an unhappy childhood or teenage years. A relationship can carry wounds and injuries for some time. However, if *both* are injured personalities, the relationship will likely deteriorate.

Of course, the above points are only warnings, and I do not want to alienate anybody from their decision. However, if you find that any of the warnings might apply to your relationship, you should take it seriously and deal with the issue right away. It is a good start to talk about such issues with your partner, but it might help even more to enlist the services of a professional therapist. Marriage is one of the most important decisions of your life, so seize every means to make the best of it!

---

* David H. Olson, John DeFrain, and Amy K. Olson, *Building Relationships: Developing Skills for Life* (Minneapolis: Life Innovations, 1999), p. 48.

3

{ spouse, domestic partner, or POSSLQ? }

One of the most prominent features of the postmodern lifestyle is to embrace freedom of choice as we consider the abundance of options now available to us. But because we must make thousands of decisions every day, that will not always be easy. Freedom to choose whatever we wish can even be a form of bondage if we find ourselves forced to make a particular choice. The same is true for relationships as well. There are several forms of relationships available, and others around us will often select them based on their own motivations.

Which one will be the best choice? Which one will most likely help us reach the happiness we've longed for? Which one offers the best guarantee for a healthy balance between individual growth and fulfilling companionship? Which one has the greatest chance to provide predictability and stability? Let's look at a range of options.

1. Marriage. Alice and Steve had been dating for two and a half years when they felt a growing desire to take their relationship to a higher level. It was clear to both of them that meant marriage. Wanting to be prepared for the big step, they searched online for "premarital counseling" and found a professional. The counselor had five meetings with them, discussed the most important areas of marriage preparation, and gave them homework. They wrote down their relational and family goals and made a family budget. Now they are in the third year of their marriage and expecting their first child. While they've had rough times during those first three years, they've managed the challenges quite well, thanks to the marriage preparation course.

I chose marriage to begin my list of symbiotic forms of relationships because it is the oldest and most tried form of them all. We find marriage, as a lifelong and committed union of two people of the opposite sex, mentioned in ancient times even before clergy or marriage officials began to officiate in it. Marriage was a family event performed in the presence of the wider society. The members of the community gathered for the ceremony, and they made the event official—the presence of the witnesses themselves formally legalized the relationship. After the first centuries of the Christian Era the right to perform a marriage ceremony became the privilege of the church. In the nineteenth century, however, Western governments, especially in Europe, started to push through legislations that would separate marriage and church weddings, making it a civil union.

Marriage is still the best form of living together. We find, for example, this illustrated by a representative survey of my own country: nearly 70 percent of the population still thinks marriage is the most ideal form of living together.

2. Domestic Partnership. The lives of Helen and George turned out to be different. They both attended the same university, and during the fourth semester they met in a course both were taking. The shared class became shared fun, and they fell in love. In time they decided to rent a flat together so that they could find peace and intimacy. They found their love sometimes shadowed by the reality of living in the same apartment, as they had to do the household chores they both disliked and occasionally had arguments about. Their friends started teasing that they behaved like an old married couple. Not so long ago George escorted home one of his cute study-group friends, Leah. Somehow they ended up in her bed after an intimate chat. Helen became quite upset, but he argued that he had never promised fidelity to her.

As the above example shows, their relationship was based on another set of principles than those of marriage. It is easier to enter such a partnership, and it is also easier to get out of it. Looking back into history, we can observe similar accounts of such partnerships, which show that this type of living together has a long tradition. For example, in the Bible we learn from Jesus' conversation with the Samaritan woman that she had five husbands, and the man with whom she was currently living was not her husband.

During the nineteenth century almost 1 percent of the population of my own country married "over the broomstick," as people called it in those days. During the twentieth century Judge Ben B. Lindsey raised the idea of a "trial marriage." In 1929 Bertrand Russell recommended it to university students, and Margaret Mead brought it to the attention of the public. By the 1960s such partnerships received a powerful impetus as the sexual revolution and the hippie movement created communes, in which a group of young people shared living quarters and beds. Nearing the millennium, many countries made the domestic partnership a legal form of cohabitation. Countries established various regulations and rules concerning the use of the family names, adoption rights, inheritance, property division, and other issues.

3. POSSLQ (*Persons of Opposite Sex Sharing Living Quarters*). Frank has just gone through an ugly divorce. His ex got custody of the children and the car, and in exchange for not paying monthly support, he even left the house for her. Basically, he is starting his life all over again. Then one of his friends introduces him to Margaret. She is also divorced but still lives in her own home, which she is renovating.

Getting to know each other is beneficial for both of them. Frank needs living quarters and a woman who sometimes prepares dinner for him, and Margaret is happy that Frank knows how to remodel the house. They sleep in separate rooms, but they are technically seeing each other. Neither wants anything serious, but if fate should bring them closer they are OK with it.

As the number of divorces increases, more and more similar situations arise. Courts generally favor the mother, thus forcing many men to leave their homes behind. The women, then, still have a very full life, but without a partner. Typically, in relationships like that of Frank and Margaret, the woman is several years older than the man, and they also maintain other relationships on the side.

Although this third type of cohabitation has spread through every Western society, I assume that the reader is not involved in it, because you intend to get married—thus I will leave it out of the comparison. Let's have a look at the different dynamics of marriage and domestic partnership, and why marriage is a more sensible decision.

Why Do Many People Choose Domestic Partnership?

The form of cohabitation a person chooses depends on many factors, including social trends, parental patterns, individual value systems, etc. But many still claim that it "just happened." The following factors appear to be the main reasons behind forming domestic partnerships:

1. A change in ethical attitudes. The moral values that have determined the dominant attitude of a society for centuries have changed during the past decades. Instead of focusing on the collective benefit, or common good, now the focus is on individual prosperity, personal interests, and the validation of needs. Research beginning in the 1990s showed that by then only 10 percent of brides were virgins, half of the women were single at the birth of their first child, and most didn't wish to marry the child's father. Furthermore, 20 percent of the firstborns in marriages were conceived before marriage, and the number of divorces per year had reached half the number of annual marriages. A therapeutic approach used more frequently in recent years, one that encourages the innocent party of an adulterous spouse to learn to accept the situation and live with it, has strengthened the trend. This concept argues that if the partners do not expect sexual fidelity from each other, they will not have to suffer disappointment.

> **20%** of the firstborns in marriages in the 1990s were conceived before marriage.

According to this school of thought, people stray because of a self-justified need, and it feels wrong only because of conventional moral condemnation. In their opinion the focus of therapeutic work is to reorganize the relationship in a way that can accept external relationships, and loyalty between the committed couple would appear in *other* areas of the relationship. The idea is that one can remove internal barriers that cause unnecessary guilt.

I myself cannot identify with this school of thought, because an extramarital affair harms the central element of marriage, namely the couple's "We" identity: their trust, intimacy, and reliance on each other. And an injury of the "We" identity is very difficult to heal. We can best illustrate the difficulty of changing morality itself with the fact that most of these cases do end in divorce.

2. The liberalization of university residence halls. While male and female college students primarily used to reside in separate buildings, today's coed buildings make it possible for them to live together during their education. This phenomenon may also play a role in those Western countries in which domestic partnerships are more common among "intellectuals."

This is exactly what happened to Nora and Peter. They lived in the dorm in adjoining corridors, but they often slept in each other's rooms, ate together, bathed together, and studied together. As fresh graduates they wanted to start a life together, but couldn't feel the same passion anymore—something they both deemed essential in a relationship. As Peter put it, it was "as if our relationship over the years had worn out." Nora thought that a person should feel much deeper feelings toward the "right one," so she expressed uncertainty in Peter being the "one" for her.

3. The time of getting sexually active and the time of getting married are growing further apart. Biologically, people can (and used to, centuries ago) be sexually mature around the ages of 15 or 16, and couples used to get married by the age of 19 or 20. Nowadays marriage commonly gets postponed until the 30s. In addition, both boys and girls reach biological maturity earlier, around the age of 12-14—thus today's young adults have to "endure" 15 years of being single during the prime period of their sexual performance, instead of the former three to five years. Consider Andrea, who studied law. In the years after university studies she didn't want to commit to anyone. She wanted to develop professionally and wished to see advancement and security at her work. Marriage or motherhood did not fit in well with her ambitions. As a result, she tried to satisfy her longing for intimacy with both casual and more serious relationships. They included one-night stands as well as more promising long-term relationships. But whenever things would begin to turn more serious, Andrea would pull out. Now at 38, she is a valued member of a law firm and attends a self-recognition course, because she cannot relate intimately to anyone. At the same time she is full of anxiety that she may never find the right one and will never experience motherhood.

4. High housing costs. If two independent young adults fall into a love relationship, it often seems financially sensible to move in together. The couple has to maintain only one residence and can spend the savings on other things. As they began planning their future life, Dora and Sam realized that by moving in together they could save a nice sum every month that they could put toward a down payment on a house. However, what initially looked like a good idea later became a burden for them, simply because the beginning of any relationship should be spent getting to know each other, cultivating intimacy and communication, and developing common goals. Rather than working on those foundational areas, Sam spent his days figuring how to share expenses or household tasks. They had little time left for relaxation and discussion, both of which have an important role in developing relationships. Instead they were burdened with tasks that were supposed to be addressed much later, and within a stronger relationship.

5. Certain legislation discriminating against married couples. In my experience certain laws have pushed people into a partnership even if they never intended to choose such cohabitation. In Europe, for example, a widow will receive certain kinds of benefits as long as she remains unmarried. Similar regulations exist in the United States, leading many elderly couples to live together unmarried. As a result, many older people live in a partnership, despite their beliefs, just to avoid losing their financial security. I have even come across a case in which a couple was legally divorced just so the wife could qualify as a single mother and receive an increased family allowance, a housing benefit, special tax incentives, and loan assistance. But the couple still lived together.

"Premarital cohabitation actually decreases the relationship satisfaction of the couple."

{spouse, domestic partner, or POSSLQ?}

The sad part of the story is that after finishing the construction of their house, the couple broke up and got into a nasty lawsuit dealing with the allocation of assets. It is worth it to rethink whether this kind of loophole-seeking relationship is appropriate. Are the monetary benefits and social help truly worth it in the long run? By giving support in certain kinds of family situations, society might inadvertently encourage individuals to be irresponsible in their relationships.

6. *Trial marriage.* In modern countries a vast percentage of the population believes that the best way to prepare for a marriage is to live together before the wedding. But research has shown that such an idea is nothing but a myth. In reality, premarital cohabitation actually *decreases* the relationship satisfaction of the couple. We could illustrate the pitfalls of "trial marriage" by the process of buying a car. If prospective buyers could take a car home and test it for a half year before purchasing it, would that increase their satisfaction after they conclude the deal? Would the prospective buyer use the car as if they already own it? Or would they plunge into dangerous situations, not sparing the engine, and not keeping it as clean, all because their feeling of responsibility is different from that of an owner? By the time the six-month trial period is over and they have to commit and make the payment, they may think twice before buying a used, rundown, dirty car (especially if they have to pay the same amount as for a new car). I believe the situation is very similar in the case of a spouse. A relationship must be lived, not taken advantage of—not "tested" or pushed to its limits just to see what they are. Coexistence without commitment promotes exploitation much more than the building of a long-term, mutually committed, safe life.

Dynamical Problems of Cohabitation

A number of psychological and sociological studies have targeted this form of relationship in the past decades, and the findings are quite sobering. For example, in cohabitation the rate of physical abuse is three times higher than in marriages,[1] as is the level of alcohol usage. Furthermore, such relationships are three to five times more prone to end than are marriages. Yet many still consider cohabitation or "trial marriage" as the best way to prepare for marriage.[2] Is it true, or is this popular opinion no more than a myth?

A typical story at first seems to support the popular position about cohabitation: "Robert and Sarah had been happily living together for five years, but when they got married, they divorced after a year." And many present such accounts as empirical proof that marriage is an outdated institution and a partnership is thus much better suited to the needs of today's generation.

What really happened in such cases? Research has revealed that a specific pattern of conflict management solidifies during the first two years of cohabitation, and the couple will continue to use this strategy until the end of the relationship. Therefore it doesn't matter if a couple is married or if they cohabitate without planning anything else for the future—the way they resolve their conflicts will take shape in the first two years of living together.[3]

Since the major difference between marriage and cohabitation is the level of commitment, it is easy to predict why Robert and Sarah might get divorced—and why the story repeats itself in other cases, too. The partners resolve their conflicts during cohabitation in a setting in which they have not fully committed themselves to each other. The possibility will always exist that in case they cannot work out a problem, one or the other can simply pack up and leave. When they finally make the decision to move their relationship to a higher level and commit to each other in a marriage, the changed status will exist only until the first marital dispute, when they will instinctively respond to each other in the way they have learned to do previously. They may easily bring the possibility of stepping out of the relationship back onto the table again, and it might quickly turn into reality. Instead of strengthening the bond, marriage will instead speed up the dynamics leading to the end of the entire relationship. The trouble is not with marriage itself, but with the fact that the couple had always lacked the level of commitment required for it.

What is the solution to the situation? In the case of Alice and Steve we can see the importance the role of premarital counseling can play in the success of a marriage. It is even truer for those who have lived together before marriage. A qualified counselor may help the couple to understand their conflict management techniques and modify them if necessary.

Recently we invited over a friend of our daughter's, along with her parents. When we were past the introductory part of the conversation, they opened up and told us a few stories about their relationship struggles, including incidents with the in-laws. At one point I asked them how long they had been married. From the strange expression on their faces I could tell that it wasn't the right question. The man eventually broke the silence and admitted that they were not married because they didn't believe in it—it was just like cohabitation, only with an extra piece of paper. In his opinion, no relationship thrives because of a piece of paper, but because of mutual love.

That is an appealing argument. And it could even be true, if not for the statistics that partnerships are three to five times more likely to break up than actual marriages. What does this "piece of paper" add, then, to the quality of the relationship?

Ultimately, we can interpret a wedding as a ritual—and rituals have played vital roles in the life of humanity since ancient times. Helping to highlight the borders between different life stages, they thus have an important function in transitioning to the new situation. The marriage ceremony, then, would make the whole family and others reconsider their attitude toward the couple. For example, they would henceforth treat their wedded children as adults and relate to them that way, as equal in status. From now on they are first spouses and second the children of their parents.

Let me clarify all this with an example. Let's assume that the grandmother in the Smith family becomes ill and is hospitalized. Doctors have a long struggle to save her life, but in the end all attempts fail. Grandmother dies. The hospital sends the following notification to the family:

"We inform you that despite the best and all available efforts, Henrietta has died. The funeral is to be provided by the hospital ex officio, so you have nothing further to worry about. Feel free to continue your lives as if nothing has happened. Sincerely, Bob Jones, CEO of Central Hospital."

I wonder how the Smith family would receive such news. Would they be relieved that they do not have to deal with a funeral? No dressing in black or notifying all the relatives? Or rather, would they insist on organizing the funeral themselves, contacting and inviting the family, and even paying the costs themselves despite the emotional stress, expenses, and weariness?

Why would they choose the second option? Because they know that the funeral and mourning are important in dealing with the grief. The funeral is a ritual that helps process the events—a landmark that closes one phase of life and helps start a new one. That is why mourning rituals used to last several days. People hired professional mourners to wail and cry, helping the relatives go through the grief and get on with their life.

I admit that the analogy is a bit morbid, but as funeral rituals play an essential role in processing grief, so wedding rituals contribute to establishing a strong, committed relationship. Such ceremonies and rituals are actually quite sophisticated. They reflect centuries of tradition and are shaped to be coded messages. Interestingly, the more we get away from rituals, the more confusion we experience in the original ideas to which the rituals serve as a reference. I especially noticed this when I spoke with a 60-year-old man on a train. He had three daughters, and I asked about their family status.

"Gabbie is the oldest. She is married and has two handsome and naughty sons. Barbara is the smallest and still studies at the university, but has a serious boyfriend."

I realized that the man left out the middle daughter, so I asked about her.

"Well, Eva, she . . . how to put it . . . lives in a relationship and has a little girl."

As the talk continued, it became clear that Eva was cohabitating, and the old man didn't quite know how to deal with the situation. On the one hand, he felt his daughter was already an independent woman with a family, while on the other, he couldn't treat her as a separate unit, and felt he was still responsible for her. And Eva cultivated this feeling also, because she had already moved home three times during difficulties in her relationship. To quote Christoph Morgenthaler, a Swiss pastoral theologian and counselor:

"The family rituals (such as a birthday celebration, a commonly eaten dinner, and much more), more or less formalized, are repetitive transaction patterns which play an important role in the success of collective life lived out in the bonds of the family. In this, family therapy and family sociology unanimously agrees."[4]

We also learn from Morgenthaler exactly which kind of role the rituals play in our lives:

- ***They protect the integrity of the family from becoming unorganized and falling apart.*** As in the case of the man on the train, for a family to interpret itself as a family unit, it needs organization and clearly drawn boundaries. If an important ritual—in our case, the wedding—gets missed, it would cause confusion in the family, who will not know exactly how to relate to its own member and his or her partner. Who is he, actually, in this family? What responsibilities does family have toward her? What responsibilities does he have toward the family? Is her family of origin still the primary immediate family for her, or does she belong to the newly created one? These and similar issues always lurk beneath the surface, begging to be answered.
- ***They strengthen the togetherness of the family members.*** It is interesting that these two rituals, the wedding and the funeral, are ones that can bring the entire family together. Everybody who matters will attend them, even on workdays, and even if they live far away. At the wedding the couple faces the large social net made up of grandparents, uncles, aunts, cousins, and other relatives, which is an important resource for them. Marriage is therefore not a private matter between two persons. It is a covenant, as it has been for centuries, and is unimaginable without witnesses and ceremonies.
- ***They establish and maintain a family identity.*** A wedding clearly indicates that the couple is not left alone. It represents a history—there are roots and continuity to pass on to the next generation. Whatever their relationship to the ancestors, they are not living in a vacuum. When they say "we," they cannot just think about the two of them, but a number of traditions, history, and anecdotes, by which the past has shaped the present.
- ***They stimulate both verbal and nonverbal communication.*** Rituals, by their very nature, are able to display things often difficult to put into words. At the same time, they elicit emotions and actions that can be hard to describe. Those present can both experience the emotions and see an illustration of what they mean and how they fit into our lives.
- ***They assist the transmission of values and rules from one generation to another.*** Information from the past can teach us lessons that help prepare for a new stage of life, one unknown until now. Values and rules play a particular role in this. The couple does not necessarily have to continue the value system of their parents and grandparents, but it will still serve as an important reference point in rethinking and articulating their own values and rules.
- ***They assist the transition from one life stage to another.*** The marriage signals a new phase for everyone. It cues the couple that they must take responsibility for their own family, but it also reminds the parents that they will no longer have the say in their children's decisions. The parents

will have to treat them as equal partners and support them from a far greater distance than before. The wedding helps to process this, allowing many emotions the freedom to express themselves. That is why we see parents overcome with emotion at so many weddings, because the ceremony helps them realize those emotions and deal with them.

- **They assist in facing nonconscious processes, which reduces the sense of fear.** The wedding, with its exact proceedings, unites the family members with all those who have traveled the same path. This in turn reduces the fear of the unknown. It conveys the assurance that many have already experienced a similar process, and everyone has found ways to deal with it. If they succeed, why should we not also?

Returning to the issue, we have established that indeed the "paper" is not what holds the marriage together. However, it is a tangible expression of an important ritual, without which the family members would be lacking vital elements needed during the formation of a new unit of their community. Naturally it does not mean that the size, budget, or number of wedding guests dictate the success of the marriage, but the harmony of several factors. Experiencing a wedding ritual is an important step toward a successful relationship. So the next time you hear someone say that marriage is only a piece of paper, feel free to protest.

---

[1] Allan V. Horwitz and Helene R. White, "The Relationship of Cohabitation and Mental Health: A Study of a Young Adult Vohort," *Journal of Marriage and the Family* 60 (1998): 505-514.

[2] Pongrácz Tiborné and Spéder Zsolt, "Élettársi kapcsolat és házasság—Hasonlóságok és különbségek az ezredfordulón," *Szociológiai Szemle* 4 (2003): 55-75.

[3] Mark A. Fine and John H. Harvey, *Handbook of Divorce and Relationship Dissolution* (Mahwah, N.J.: Lawrence Erlbaum, 2006), p. 205.

[4] Christoph Morgenthaler, *Systemische Seelsorge* (Stuttgart: Kohlhammer, 2005), p. 189.

{marriage preparation:}
why, how, with whom, and for how much?

Premarital Counseling: Why?

Although marriage is a private matter of two persons, its quality also affects those around them and ultimately, though it sounds commonplace, it touches everyone. The annual amount society has to pay for the medical treatment of physical abuse victims or increased benefits for parents and children left alone because of divorce goes well into the billions. Furthermore, the children who grow up in broken families will have similar behavioral patterns in their relationships—not to mention that each month women and children die from acts of domestic violence.

Society is willing to take precautions in other areas of life in which a potential for harm has much shorter-term effects and is more visible. Consider driving a car.

Since a car can cause serious damage if the driver is poorly trained or reckless, society requires its members to complete a long and costly learning program before it allows someone to drive without supervision. Before we let a person venture into traffic he or she must show skills in first aid, know the highway code, participate in driver's ed, and then pass a test that confirms the candidate possesses the necessary knowledge and skills to safely operate the car. All this lasts several months (if the person succeeds the first time around), and it can be a costly process.

> It is important to realize that marriage preparation is not designed to prove whether or not the couple fits together.

But that is only for obtaining the license. The driver can expect at any moment that a smiling, uniformed police officer will knock on the window and check his or her license, the car, and his or her ability to drive. Everything will be fine if he or she has put the rules learned during driver's ed into practice. And if he or she does make a mistake (depending on the nature and magnitude of the error), appropriate social discipline will be given (fine, citation, etc.), or for larger violations of traffic laws, the authorities may prohibit the individual from operating a car, or require a revisit of a driver's course.

To gain a marriage license, however (and marriage is no less dangerous than driving a car), an ID card and birth certificate are usually sufficient. The couple presents them to a clerk, has them verified, and then has a short waiting period (except in Las Vegas).

After the wedding, no one asks (except in small talk) if the marriage is working fine. There are no roadside checks, and if someone causes an accident (a divorce), then the person has only to present a court order at the next wedding, indicating the legal ending of his or her previous marriage.

Marriage preparation ends this anomaly.

Fortunately, more and more countries are recognizing the need to require the completion of a marriage preparation program for couples. Almost everyone is in love on the wedding day, and almost everybody starts the marriage with an intention that it will never end. But the 45 percent[1] divorce rate is sobering. It shows that marriage can go wrong, and that the couples were most likely not well enough prepared. Therefore, in developed societies with premarital counseling programs, couples can seek the help of a trained counselor. Marriage preparation has several schools and methods that have been tested by scientific research and efficacy studies. I know of even a case in which such a program reduced the divorce rate to below 2 percent through a combination of premarital counseling and mentoring![2] Compared to the 45 percent level, a 2 percent rate is quite striking.

Such preparation may be particularly important for those getting ready for a second or third wedding. They tend to believe that in the previous marriage(s) they have learned enough to maintain a better relationship in the future. However, as the previous divorce indicates, they possess setbacks and now ingrained habits that they need to overcome for the sake of the next marriage. Statistics reveal that the second or more marriages are even more in danger of ending in a divorce than was the first marriage.

Also, couples that have lived together for a longer time should seriously consider marriage preparation, because—as we saw previously—the dynamics of marriage and cohabitation are different, and they need to be aware of this. If they lived together before the marriage for close to two years, their conflict management style has already taken shape according the dynamics of the cohabitation, and they will carry it into the marriage itself. Since the two forms of relationships are different in so many aspects, serious problems can easily appear soon into the marriage. The pillars of marriage are intimacy, passion, and commitment. During conflicts, however, such couples will behave as if they were not ultimately committed to each other. Thus, it is only a matter of time.

Marriage Preparation: How?

During the counseling process the counselor assesses the couple's relationship and explores their different areas of strength and growth (I deliberately will not talk about a weakness, because stumbling blocks can be turned into stepping-stones). Then, during five to eight sessions the expert will provide an opportunity to discuss issues that the couple has not yet sorted out. A couple could have many repressed disagreements that they have locked away for the sake of peace. The presence of an experienced counselor will enable them to resolve the issues constructively, without unforgiving feelings. If the couple gets into a deadlock, the facilitator will use exercises to move on and arrive at a solution. He or she will give special attention to communication style, conflict resolution abilities, and how the couple treats the differences in their personalities. These are the areas that can make or break the relationship, affecting the couple's ability to tackle life's challenges confidently. In addition, an analysis of the family of origin is an important part of the preparation. It will particularly explore two main areas: the flexibility of the relationship and the emotional attachment of family members. Not only is this important so that the couple will be able to detach themselves from their parents, making their marriage the most important tie in their life, but because when under pressure, people naturally revert to the "old style" they experienced as teens at home. If the two styles are very different, things will need processing and resolving. Since this can take a long time, premarital counseling should ideally start six months before the wedding.

However, it is important to realize that marriage preparation is not designed to prove whether or not the couple fits together. The two involved must alone make that decision. But the program can help them a great deal to move up one or two stars and have a vitalized, well-functioning marriage and to become more conscious of and considerate in their relationship.

All over the world more and more counselors use the PREPARE program, which contains all the important relationship dimensions and can produce a very precise inventory of the couple's relationship. It returns a 15-page report that will enable the counselor to design the sessions according to the needs of each individual couple. Administered to more than 3 million pairs worldwide, the test has become the most popular and most reliable relationship assessment tool.

Another option is a group program with relationship training. Conducted with six to 12 couples preparing for marriage, it can be either an intensive weekend program or a longer series with weekly sessions. It allows couples to learn from one another. Of course, one can combine the two methods for those who seek the utmost preparation. You can explore both methods at www.prepare-enrich.com, where you can select a facilitator or choose a group program.

Another great way of preparing is the internationally available online method, the Couple Checkup. It is a user-friendly form of PREPARE that you can complete online, even without the help of a counselor. Both parties need to answer a few series of questions and immediately after finishing, a 20- to 25-page document will be e-mailed to them with a detailed inventory of the couple's relationship. Such an inventory highlights several factors of the relationship of long-term importance. However, the couple has not yet discussed them with each other. In each category the document indicates if it is a strength or growth area in the relationship and provides suggestions on how to consciously improve it. Building on more than 40 years of research, this method has become highly reliable.

After completing the Couple Checkup, you can certainly decide to seek help from a trained counselor. You just have to e-mail the inventory report to the chosen therapist, and he or she will be able to incorporate it into the sessions. The program is available in English at www.couplecheckup.com.

Marriage Preparation: With Whom?

After realizing the importance of premarital counseling, you next have to know whom to turn to. A psychologist or therapist may come to mind, but after contacting one, the professional may likely ask what your "problem," "issue," or "concern" might be. You may become slightly taken aback by this introduction, as your intention of getting married is not a disease or a mental illness! Of course some therapists do work from a preventative mind-set and not only deal with existing problems. You can certainly get help from them in your marital preparation.

The other option is the wide range of clergy professionals. Premarital counseling is a part of every theological curriculum. Prospective priests and pastors learn much more about marriage preparation than any other professional. One should discover as much as possible about the qualifications of the pastor, however, because many sessions with clergy go only as far as "good moral counsel" and discussing details of the wedding ceremony.

So who is ultimately the best choice for premarital counseling? As the brief summary above suggests, marriage preparation is not explicitly a psychotherapeutic process (since psychotherapy starts with illness, turmoil, or a symptom as a starting point), but neither is it entirely a theological job, as the theologian primarily addresses the transcendent—not its daily life application. I like to classify premarital counseling as "psycho-educative"[3] counseling in which helpers can contribute equally with psychological or theological background. This new approach is becoming a more popular and independent psychological specialty (www.prepare-enrich.com and www.couplecheckup.com have representatives of every profession available).

Finally, an increasing number of programs are now offered that are not conducted by practitioners, but by lay couples. They emphasize more the sharing of experiences than discussing exact, science-based information. Such programs are very helpful in providing insight for the best ways to prepare, though it is smart to investigate beforehand their quality and their ideological background, and also check to see if they have an efficiency study.

Marriage Preparation: For How Much?

It would be unfair to present this subject without saying a few words about costs. We know that if something is valuable, it should come at a price. People tend not to value things provided for free. The professionals have expenses that their clients will eventually pay, such as the counselors' continuous education, fees for administered tests, office operation, etc. However, this need not dampen your enthusiasm about marriage preparation. Consider the expenses as an investment in your relationship! In addition, many organizations (such as churches and NGOs [nongovernmental organizations]) will partly or fully take over the costs from the couple. If money is a problem for you, look into this option. Many church communities honestly believe in the long-range effects of a solid marriage and are ready to selflessly support any engaged couple in properly preparing for it.

---

[1] Full divorce rate in my home country during 2007. Other Western nations have equivalent levels.

[2] The program was based on PREPARE, the seven sessions of marriage preparation was complemented by a marriage mentoring program under the direction of Pastor Robert Oglesby in a church in Texas (director, Center for Youth and Family Ministry, Abilene Christian University, 242 Biblical Studies Building, Abilene, Texas 79699). Mentors were licensed PREAPRE/ENRICH facilitators. From the 320 participating couples only four got divorced, but 60 couples decided during the preparation process not to get married. Source: https://www.prepare-enrich.com/webapp/pe_main/mainsite/research/template/DisplaySecureContent.vm;pc=1270105897751?id=pe_main_site_content*pages*research*public*MarriageMentorStudiesInfo.html&xlat=Y&emb_org_id=0&emb_prp_id=0&emb_unq_id=0&emb_lng_code=ENGLISH.

[3] Andreas Bochmann, *Praxisbuch Ehevorbereitung: Anregungen für Seelsorge und Beratung* (Giessen, Basel: Brunnen, 2004), p. 20.

5

{ the goal of marriage: *1+1=1* }

How do you bake a good marriage? You might wonder, but I deliberately formulated this—perhaps at the first reading—in a slightly silly way. Marriage is, in some senses, similar to the baking of the bread (without denying the previous metaphor I used of gardening). If you have baked bread, you will know exactly what I mean.

Bread needs several ingredients that do not resemble the final product, either in color (like flour), consistency (water), scent (yeast), or taste (salt). But the adequate mixture of the materials and the right process (kneading, rising, baking) will produce the desired outcome: tasty, nutritious bread. The same is true for marriage. A good marriage involves a set of components that at first glance do not show any resemblance to the final product. But mix and process accordingly, and they will return the desired outcome: a happy, lifelong marriage. The following chapters will closely examine those elements.

Icebreaker Questions:
- What will change in your relationship after the wedding, and what will be the same?
- What does the ideal balance between "we" and "I" look like in your relationship?
- Is it possible that you will experience problems in your marriage that will put your commitment to the test?

One beautiful, symbolic act of the marriage ceremony involves the couple lighting a common candle and blowing out their individual candlesticks. It indicates that the two lives are united from now on and the two "I"s becomes a "we." This is one of the most important goals of a marriage. John M. Gottman observes that "happy marriages are based on a deep friendship. By this I mean a mutual respect for and enjoyment of each other's company. These couples tend to know each other intimately—they are well versed in each other's likes, dislikes, personality quirks, hopes, and dreams. They have an abiding regard for each other and express this fondness not just in the big ways but also in little ways, day in and day out."[1] Then he adds: "They don't just 'get along'—they also support each other's hopes and aspirations and build a sense of purpose into their lives together."[2]

Given the importance of the issue, let me quote a few other excellent professionals about what it means to become "we."

According to Diana S. Garland, "when spouses are equipped in this manner, they can build a strong, flexible relationship that changes over time as their needs change, and that enhances the personal growth of each partner within the marriage."[3]

David Mace, pioneer of the Marriage Enrichment movement, states: "Intimacy simply means opening up to another person the areas of our personal lives which we normally conceal out of fear that airing these areas could make them vulnerable to attack."[4]

So what is the ultimate purpose of marriage? Somewhat philosophically, in the footsteps of Kant, I would say: *The relationship is not a tool to achieve a goal, but it is the goal itself.* The goal of a marriage is to form the "we" out of the two "I"s, with a common language, value system, and culture.

What can help the couple to shape a common life? The answer is almost self-evident: love. However, each might not have the same understanding of the term. There are many things we say we love, yet the word means something different in every situation. I love my wife, but I love football, too. I love my car, but I also love pancakes. I love my kids, but I love my parrots as well. Do I mean exactly the same in every case?

{the goal of marriage}

Former Yale University professor Robert J. Sternberg[5] helps to resolve the dilemma. According to his research, three aspects of love must appear in a marriage in order for it to last long. The marriage relationship differs from all other human love of persons or objects, because the parties make conscious efforts to express *all three* aspects of love in high-quality ways. The first area of love is the physical one, **passion,** which includes attraction, sexual desires, and the intense yearning to be united with the other. (Note: An active sexual life is not a *condition* of the existence or experience of passion, but I will revisit that later.) The second characteristic concerns more of the feeling of belonging or **intimacy,** the emotional part of love. The third element of love is the cognitive side that will help a couple stay together in both good and bad times, and we call it **commitment**. All three are necessary in a marriage. If any one of them is missing, the relationship will lose its strength and become unbalanced.

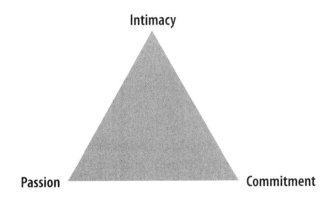

So what happens when one aspect of love is missing? Let us examine all the options:

Intimacy + Passion = Romantic Love

Such a type of relationship lacks commitment. Its participants enjoy their affair when life is good to them, but under pressure it will probably grow cold, because their relationship is not a conscious decision. Rather, it is based on mutual romantic emotions. There is nothing romantic about a quarrel, a conflict with the in-laws, or a financial crisis. This kind of love is typical in the first phase of cohabitations. (Maybe this is one of the reasons cohabitations are three to five times more prone to a breakup.)[6] Also it is the type of relationship that married persons experience when they first enter into an affair outside of their marriage. Everything seems so easy in the extramarital relationship: no quarrels, no bills to pay, no "headaches." Everything seems so intimate, romantic, and unbelievable, until . . .

Let's see the next combination:

Intimacy + Commitment = Friendship

When I meet with such couples, I soon get a feeling that something is missing. They are extremely correct, very nice, courteous, and respectful to each other. Yet something is missing. I cannot see the spark in their eyes. I do not get the impression that they would be willing to burst through walls for each other. Recently I saw just such a pair. After an introduction the man told me: "We decided to get married. Would you prepare us for marriage?" He said it without emotion on his face, with a tone as if he spoke about his workplace.

Passion + Commitment = Unfulfilled Love

Extreme emotional swings are characteristic to these relationships. The famous "love at first sight," its parties have an idealistic picture of each other and are actually in love with the image, not the real person. It will be a huge disappointment when they realize that the other one is quite different than what they imagine.

Thus we need all three aspects of love in a relationship in order to love someone wholly and long-term.

Intimacy + Passion + Commitment = Fulfilled, Lasting Relationship

The Spell of Rose-colored Glasses

We must address one more issue in relation to the goal of the marriage. The greatest disappointments have often a very simple reason: surreal goals. Most married couples experience this during the first couple years of their relationship. Lack of knowledge, or "rose-colored glasses," leads them to create goals that do not meet the reality of life, and therefore will inevitably fail. Here is a short list of goals you had better *not* set, because you cannot reach them (and believe me, they are not enjoyable if forced):

- ***Most of our problems will be resolved after marriage.*** False! Getting married does not involve brainwashing and is not a magic solution. If you have problems now, you should process and solve them right away. If you cannot work them out, then ask yourself honestly if you still want to marry.

- ***My partner meets all my needs.*** False! You will still need friends, because your spouse will not be able to be a partner in absolutely everything you like. A man will always require male friends with whom he can discuss "manly" things, and a woman will always seek female friends, with whom she can enjoy "girls-night/day-out"-type activities.

- ***If you really love each other, you can sense what the other wants.*** Nonsense! But in particular, women tend to support this expectation toward the new husband. Believe me—no matter how much you love each other, you will never become mind readers! The other party will know your desires only when you speak up. And it is unfair to expect something that the other one cannot fulfill. The inability to read minds and determine wishes is *not* a sign that the person doesn't love enough—it is an indication of ineffective communication. "If you don't ask, you don't get."¹

- **We will never have serious differences in our marriage.** Such has never occurred in reality. The life of every family has problems and tension that they need to address. The changes of life cycle can especially make for a sensitive time for the couple (such as the birth of a child, raising school-age children, job shifts, etc.). With all of them come tensions and conflicts that must be resolved. Wherever people live in close proximity it is natural to experience disagreements, conflicts of interest, and differences in taste.

> "Happy marriages are based on a deep friendship. By this I mean a mutual respect for and enjoyment of each other's company."

- **My love toward my partner will never falter.** In periods of crisis emotions will be too heated to rely on, so these are the times that commitment will help overcome differences. Afterward, however, you will feel much closer than before. It is worth it to hang on!

- **In a good marriage the partners do everything together.** Please, not this! Becoming "we" doesn't mean that the newlywed couple cannot even breathe without each other. They will need to maintain a healthy balance between time spent together and apart.

- **Change can be dangerous, and we should try to keep our life as it is.** Every situation in life is different and requires its own strategy for resolution, and certainly this makes change essential. Many make the mistake of using only one kind of problem-solving technique and forcing it in every situation, whether it is truly suitable or not. Even good marriages face constant changes, and couples must encourage each other to adapt to the new circumstances. It is important, however, that they progress in the same direction. If one party begins to change and the other one stays the same, it will cause a rift between them. Several times I encountered a situation in which one party went to therapy to deal with the relationship problems, and as a result her or his attitude started to change, but the other party got left behind and the gap between them grew so wide that it cost their marriage. Change is good! But do it consciously, in a concentrated and cooperative way, so that both of you can move in the same direction.

Now, I didn't write this to break your spirits. My intention is to help you find realistic expectations that will be achievable, can strengthen your relationship, and will lead you closer in happiness and success.

Exercise: We Love Each Other *T-H-I-S* Much!

To deepen your understanding of the three aspects of love, finish the sentences below, and when you both are ready, share them with each other.

1. **I can see your commitment toward me when . . .**

The bride's response: _____

_____

The groom's response: _____

_____

2. **I see the passion in your eyes when . . .**

   The bride's response: _____

   _____

   The groom's response: _____

   _____

3. **Intimacy means to me:**

   The bride's response: _____

   _____

   The groom's response: _____

   _____

After reading what each other has written, discuss the following questions:

1. *What does my partner's response bring to my own mind?*
2. *To what extent are the three aspects of love present in our life? Can we keep them in balance?*
3. *What can I alter so that my partner will feel more secure in receiving my love?*
4. *What kind of change do I want to see in the way my partner expresses her/his love for me?*

Dream Your Goals!

Now is the time to formulate your own goals for your relationship. No one can do this but you. It is your life, your dream, your marriage, and there's something very reassuring in this: No one knows your relationship as well as you two. For this reason, you are the best experts to set your goals.

{the goal of marriage}

1. On a separate piece of paper, write down how you envision your life in 10 years: your profession, parenting situation/style, your marriage, finances, and any other area you find important. Be as specific as you can.

2. Swap papers with your partner and compare each other's goals.

3. Discuss the following questions:
    - *How do I see myself fitting into the goals of my partner?*
    - *What are our expectations for our shared life?*
    - *How do our personal goals fit with our common goals?*
    - *What can we do together to help to achieve those individually set goals?*

---

[1] John M. Gottman and Nan Silver, *The Seven Principles for Making Marriage Work* (Three Rivers Press, New York, 1999), pp. 19, 20.

[2] *Ibid.*, p. 23.

[3] Diana S. R. Garland, *Working With Couples for Marriage Enrichment* (San Francisco: Jossey-Bass Publishers, 1983), p. 2.

[4] David Mace: *Love and Anger in Marriage: How to Manage Your Conflicts* (Grand Rapids: Zondervan, 1982), p. 57.

[5] Robert J. Sternberg, "Triangulating Love," in Robert J. Sternberg, ed., *Psychology of Love* (New Haven: Yale University Press, 1988), pp. 119-138.

[6] Ákos Tárkányi, "A második demográfiai átmenet néhány főbb tényezője a fejlett világban és Magyarországon," *Demográfia* 4 (2008).

6

{ communication: }
the art of listening

Icebreaker Questions:
- When did you truly feel understood by your partner?
- What did your partner do to bring about this feeling?
- Evaluate yourselves on a scale of 1 to 10: How good are you at listening? What can you do to become better listeners?

When it comes to the word "communication," we quickly associate it with the Internet, mobile phones, and the fast-expanding world of technical media. We might also think of the communication training sessions that we had to attend at our workplaces, things that businesses believe to be good for customer relations and for improving efficiency and profit. The word "communication," however, comes from the same root as the word "community" (Latin *communio*). Marriage is community, and if we apply the original idea of the word, we can conclude that *"communication is the interaction of two persons that creates and regulates community."*[1]

Both parts of the definition are important. First, communication initially forms the community of the two persons. Second, it regulates their established community and determines its direction, frame, and rules. For this reason, if I had to pick one topic out of this book and emphasize its importance, it would be communication. It is the key to improving all other aspects of marriage. If a couple has financial problems, they can address them only through clear, intentional communication between them. Similarly, a quarrel about a mother-in-law or about disciplining the children can be resolved successfully only if they have adequate communication skills and can apply them.

> As a general rule, "What you *do* is so loud that I cannot hear what you *say!*"

The Mental Process of Communication

When two persons engage in a conversation, one usually has a message he or she wishes to convey. Appearing first in the brain in the form of images, words, ideas, feelings, or wishes, it can be influenced by mood, by the recently experienced emotions of the *other* person (sympathy, rejection, etc.), the environment around the couple, and several other factors. And since the other person can't read minds, he or she needs to articulate the message in a way that the partner can understand. In other words, the brain then encodes its electronic signals into audible and visible ones, making it possible to send the message to the other person. The other individual can now receive the message and sift it through his or her own filter of thoughts, emotions, mood, and past experience with the chatting partner. Then he or she can form an idea about the sender's intent—in other words, decrypting the message or converting the acoustic signals back into electronic ones. The following graphic depicts the process of transmitting a message:

Ideally, the receiver will see the same message in the mind's eye as what the sender intended to transmit. In reality, however, it very rarely works in such an idyllic manner. Encoding and decoding generally gets distorted along the way.

As shown in the illustration on page 47, such common communication distortion can lead to misunderstandings, and the partners might feel the other one is not truly listening. If we are in a more superficial relationship, we do not pay much importance to such communication distortion. But if in the most important relationship of our lives we repeatedly find that we are not able to successfully explain ourselves to the other, it could in the long term mean the end of the relationship. The biggest challenge of marriage is, then, to communicate in the most accurate way possible, seeking to filter out distortions.

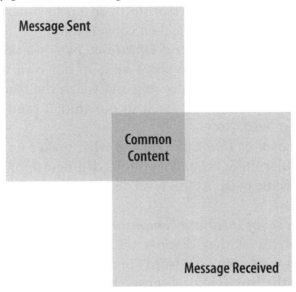

An important principle in clear communication is that we should not limit it to words only. In a conversation of two persons, words carry only 7 percent of the message. Intonation (38 percent) and body language (55 percent) contain a significantly larger part of the information. So if you want to understand each other, listen not only to what the other says but also to the intonation and body language (38 percent + 55 percent = 93 percent). As a general rule: "What you *do* is so loud that I cannot hear what you *say*!"

Levels of Communication

Communication plays a decisive role in formulating a deep, intimate "we" connection in a marriage. But such deep connection supposes an ultimate openness on a level unparalleled in other relationships. Happy couples have a common attribute: they have learned to communicate at the deepest level.

What do I mean by levels? Bryan Craig,[2] an Australian marriage expert, lists five levels (based on concepts developed by psychologist John Joseph Powell) on which we make contact with people around us. Each level is a step toward the inner core of our personality. The deeper the level, the greater the insight that we allow the other person to see about us. At the same time, as we become more vulnerable at such deeper levels, the relationship will also become more intimate.

Level 5: Cliché Level. At this stage people do not disclose anything personal. Instead, they stick with clichés or hide behind questions. Typical questions are "What's up?" "How was your day?" and the like. Discussions are usually short, shallow, and impersonal. Those who communicate primarily at this level in their marriage will soon find themselves frustrated, feeling that their relationship is empty and cold.

Level 4: The Level of Facts. Similarly, this one belongs to courtesy discussions and involves phrases behind which it is easy for people to hide their actual opinions. It does not require a person to open up to others, as it consists of strictly factual and emotionally detached conversation.

Level 3: The Level of Ideas and Opinions. Now we take the first step of opening ourselves up. We begin to share some of our own views, a small part of ourselves. At this stage we usually stop and watch the reactions of the other individual, and if the person takes well to our initial, cautious unfolding, we move on to the next level.

Level 2: The Level of Emotion. Here is what makes us individual human beings. Our particular thoughts and emotions distinguish us from all other humans—they are specific to us. At this level deep, honest, and open conversations evolve.

Level 1: The Level of Intimate Communication. Whoever opens up at this level risks vulnerability as they disclose the deepest chambers of their being. Perhaps the reason we employ the word "intimacy" to refer to sexual closeness is that it means, in the psychological sense, the nakedness of the human soul. If it happens in a safe atmosphere in which mutual acceptance occurs, this level of communication becomes an inexhaustible resource of marriage. Truly happy couples often meet each other at this level.

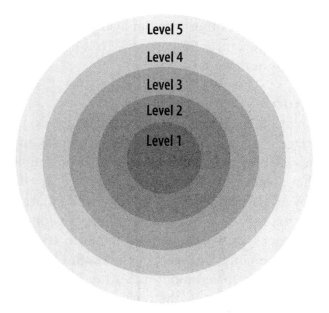

At this point I need to point out a common mistake. Many people (particularly those working in middle or upper management) attend training sessions in communication, negotiating, or assertiveness at the workplace. It is easy to assume that the methods learned in such programs will also work in their marriage, and they start using them at home—but it will lead to some very unpleasant results, because communication in a marriage has entirely different rules and goals than in business. Marriage and business communications take place at completely different levels. Business communication ranges between the fifth and third levels, and it is neither intended for nor interested in moving beyond those stages. If it does, it has fatal consequences for the relationship. Unfortunately the so-called team building exercises actually contribute to the growing divorce statistics. For example, some colleagues may go on a workplace retreat and get intimately close in a top wellness center, where they have dinner together and then go into a sauna together, supposedly to boost camaraderie and efficiency. Usually during that time the spouse is home, maybe taking care of the kids and the household alone, and by the time the other arrives home from the weekend, he or she will not seem quite as witty and fit as the colleagues at the retreat.

In the case of a good marriage, communication takes place between the third and first levels. The relationship of two persons becomes closer if they meet more often at deeper levels. If they communicate only on external levels, they will behave not as spouses, but as business acquaintances. It is important, therefore, to handle every human relationship in its right place and at the appropriate level of communication.

Toward, Away, and Against

Aside from the level of self-disclosure that the relationship has reached, another important indicator of the quality of a couple's communication is how the partners *react* to each other's self-disclosure. John M. Gottman[3] observed that we can sort the responses of a couple into three groups: toward, away, and against.

- ***Toward:*** This kind of answer brings the parties closer and facilitates discussion. Such responses indicate that they value and want to be in harmony with each other. A "toward" communication can be a kind facial gesture or a simple "yes" or "h'mmm" while the other one is speaking. They express interest and show that the person is listening.

A detailed answer can also be qualified as "toward." For example, if a wife asks her husband how his day went, he can reply: "Great! Amazingly, everything went smoothly. Even more, Pete is better and is back to work." This is better than just, "Oh, fine . . ."

- ***Away:*** Answers of this type indicate that an individual is pulling out of the conversation, and thus symbolically out of the relationship. The person ignores the other one's attempts to connect. The obstacle that turns "away" from the partner can be a cut-off response. For example, a wife wants to start a conversation with her husband, who is watching TV, and he replies, "Not now!" Or a partner might just ignore the attempts at communication, such as a wife continuing to read a book and not replying. It can also be an interrupting or

{communication}

subject-changing response, such as a wife complaining how bad the service was in a certain shop, and the husband just saying, "Could you pass the salt?"

- **Against:** A person who uses the "against" reaction does respond, but in a negative way. This kind of answer carries disrespect, and the other person feels hurt or degraded, getting the idea that neither they nor the relationship matters. Among the "against" responses belong answers that are insulting, belligerent, dominating, critical, or defensive. If a man says, "I had such a difficult day!" and his wife answers, "Do you think I've been on a picnic? All day I worked like a slave," then he feels negated.

The following table summarizes how specific responses affect a relationship:[4]

	Turning toward	Turning away	Turning against
How it affects relationships	More bidding and responding Growth and development of relationship	Less bidding Increased conflict Hurt feelings, loss of confidence Relationship ends sooner rather than later	Less bidding Avoidance of conflict Relationship ends, but it may take a while

A person does not need to be an expert to realize that a good marriage should contain a mostly "toward" communication. Few would guess, though, that responses containing "against" answers do not damage the relationship as much as the "away" responses. Negative communication is better than none. Marriage counselors say that while plates are flying (the plates, of course, are symbolic), the marriage can be saved. But if days or weeks go by with the parties not saying a word to each other, then little can be done.

It is always important to express how much we value our mate's attempts to connect. There are certain situations in which it isn't easy to be kind, and it takes serious effort to say something positive—or to apologize. But if the other party repays the effort with "away" or "against" responses, the marriage will find itself in great danger. That makes the one who opened up feel that her or his trust has been abused. Unfortunately, the partner will learn from this experience that they should never again make themselves so vulnerable. The emotionally injured person will attack back even when she or he would rather hug the other one.

I once worked with a couple who masterfully cultivated this kind of game. They used a wide selection of terms to insult each other, even in the presence of the therapist. Several times they nearly got into a physical fight. After I realized what was happening between them, I made them an offer.

"You seem to be locked up in a deadly game," I said. "You are staring each other into the eyes and have guns in your hands. You have emptied half of the bullets into each other, but you still have plenty. There is only one solution I can conceive of: One of you should make a decision not to use the gun again, put it down . . . even if the other one still has theirs and is employing it. If you can do this, then we can help you."

The man replied first: "I am not willing to do this."

And his wife was quick to reply, "Then neither will I!"

Unfortunately they are no longer a married couple. Their example illustrates that the fate of a quarrel—or a marriage—will often rest on how one party reacts to the peace initiative of the other one. Do not forget: Making yourself vulnerable is an important part on the road to intimacy, and such vulnerability should never be abused!

The Magic Ratio

As seen in the previous section, all marriages have positive and negative communication patterns. Maintaining the stability of marriage, however, depends on whether we succeed in keeping in balance the ratio of such positive and negative communication. (And by balance I do not mean a 50-50 ratio!) Gottman's research clearly demonstrated that a happy marriage maintains a five-to-one ratio of positive and negative communication.[5] In other words, if you want to live happily together for a long time, you have to give five times the compliments or praise that you do blame or criticism! The marriage will maintain its stability as long as the couple displays five times more positive emotions and messages than negative ones.

As long as this equilibrium persists, no anger, conflict, or external factors can challenge the relationship. The positive aspect can involve acts of tenderness, interest in the partner's life, expression of appreciation, empathy, unconditional acceptance, or shared joking and laughter. Because negative responses are all too well known, I will not bring up examples. The point is this: See to it that you give each other five times as much good as bad. Maybe this will seem unnatural at first, but over time it will become so much a part of your relationship that it will feel as if you have always done it.

During one marriage enrichment training event I asked half the couples to carry out a conversation about an imaginary home renovation. Then I requested the other half to watch the first group's conversations and record all positive and negative communication patterns. Afterward we calculated the average of negative and positive gestures and sentences. The result was five to four in favor of pos-

In a conversation of two persons, words carry only 7 percent of the message.

itive statements. Then the other pairs (who acted as observers) had to conduct an imaginary conversation about a car purchase. This time the first group took notes. This session's result was five to two.

Why was the latter result better than the previous? Because the second group of couples knew what to watch for. They were aware that the others were counting positive and negative messages, so they paid attention to their words.

> Communication development is very important in a marriage, but it is best if the parties develop the skills together, simultaneously.

Now you can see the importance of positive communication, and I hope you will be conscious of the fact that you have to intentionally say more positive things to each other.

Passive, Aggressive, or Assertive?

To end this chapter, let us examine communication styles. On the basis of how we think, speak, and behave, all of us belong to one of the following categories: passive, aggressive, or assertive.

- ***Passive:*** A passive person is usually uncertain. As a result, he or she is always the victim of stronger people, situations, and circumstances. He or she is the doormat of the whole world. Such people do not dare to stand up for their own interests and rather suffer as underdogs. This type endures everything: injustice, humiliation, ridicule. They automatically subordinate themselves to others, don't have personal opinions, and cannot act independently. A common motto would be "Let's hope that I will someday be given what I want. Until then, I'll hide my feelings and not let anybody know about them. I hope that others will figure out what I want on their own."

- ***Aggressive:*** This type of person is the other extreme. They do not care about the feelings, rights, or needs of others. In order to reach their goals, they are ready to sacrifice anything. They deem even human relationships as important only if they can assist their interests. Such individuals feel they are above others and express this attitude through arrogant behavior and body language and gladly show off any status symbols they possess. Their motto might be: "Get what you want, by whatever means, at any price! Ignore the feelings of others and don't consider their interests."

- ***Assertive:*** The third type represents a happy medium. Such a person can express emotions, wishes, and thoughts without offending the other party's feelings, desires, and ideas. He or she is looking for solutions that will also be acceptable to the other party. An assertive's motto is: "Both our needs are important—therefore, let's find a solution that satisfies both of us."

The chart on page 53 summarizes the characteristics of the three types:[6]

Now we will go one step further. Perhaps you've already guessed to which group you personally belong. But what is the interaction pattern of you two as a combination? What kind of marriage results when two passive people live together? What if an insecure and an aggressive meet? What about two assertive types? David H. Olson's research can provide an answer:[7]

	Passive	**Assertive**	**Aggressive**
Voice	still, vague, jerky	loud, clear, audible	shouting, agitated
Composition	insecure, uncertain, inaccurate, dim	precise, accurate, valid	attacking, offending, threatening, menacing
Content	unnecessary explanations; does not communicate needs; does not express emotions or only in indirect ways (gestures); speaks in general terms without a definite subjective	uses necessary explanation; expresses needs; speaks in first person ("I")	does not give a reason; threatens, offends; does not want to compromise; structures sentences around "you"
Body Language	afraid, withdrawing, rigid; no eye contact	lively, relaxed posture; eye contact	threatening, heated gestures; abuses eye contact: too little or too much
Result	martyr, does not achieve the personal goal	successful, respects the other's rights	bully, achieves goals by hurting others

As the table below clearly shows, pairs of assertive persons are the most satisfied in their relationship. Such partners experience a steady growth and can handle life's various challenges in a way that makes both feel like winners. Intimacy is at the highest level in their relationship.

Person A Communication Style	Person B Communication Style	Relationship	Who Wins	Level of Intimacy
passive	passive	devitalized	both lose	low
passive	aggressive	dominating	1 wins, 1 loses	low
aggressive	aggressive	conflicted	both lose	low
assertive	passive	frustrated	both lose	low
assertive	aggressive	confrontational	both lose	low
assertive	assertive	vitalized	both win	high

{communication}

Which types connect in your relationship? Of course, everyone would like to belong to the table's bottom row. If, however, only one of you—or even neither of you—falls into the assertive group, it means only that you have to work a bit harder than others. Assertiveness is a learned skill! Nobody is born confident, insecure, or aggressive, but the parents' example, experiences that form the personality, social reinforcements, and other effects can mold a person. If you know how an assertive person behaves, you can begin to imagine how they would resolve a certain situation. Then you can begin to imitate such behavior in your own life. You can start with using "I feel . . ." statements in your speech, the first-person singular instead of the aggressive "you" or a passive "a certain person" structure. It is important, however, to go through such a significant change together, one that will affect both the personality and the relationship. For example, it might be good to read a book together about assertive communication.

I have observed in a number of couples that the personality development of one spouse, whether gained from training or individual therapy, soon changed the rules in their marriage that they used to follow. It alienated them for a time, until they could develop a new balance in their relationship. The developing party often begins to overwhelm the other, which might undermine the sense of belonging. As Jürg Willi, a Swiss couple therapist, puts it: "When one party dominates the relationship sphere at the other party's expense, or the other will not observe the boundaries anymore, then the whole of the relationship will deteriorate. The distance—started with a common effort—will continue to grow: both will be losers."[8]

This is my next problem with workplace communication trainings. Teaching self-confidence and assertiveness is a major part of such programs, but at the same time they have no regard for the participants' current relationship systems. They treat the participants as if they existed and communicated only in their work environment. Communication development is very important in a marriage, but it is best if the parties develop the skills together, simultaneously. If only one of them does and the other gets left behind, it will create a distance between them. In addition, the person involved in the training will be tempted to use the newly acquired knowledge (for example, a technique to convince or sell). However, they will soon discover that a communication technique used successfully in business life will not bring the same results in marriage. Essential dynamic differences exist between the two situations (see chart on page 55).

I hope you are convinced how important communication is for marriage. You might already have a hunch as to whether this area is a strength in your relationship, or whether you need to develop it more. If you are strong in your communication, you can celebrate! It is an ability that will be very useful in other areas of your relationship. Or did some of you get a feeling that communication is a bit of a stumbling block in your relationship? But remember: Isn't the stumbling block also good for something? *To turn it into a stepping-stone* in order to reach higher!

	Business Communication	Communication in Marriage
Goals	to represent interests; to secure claims	to communicate needs; to preserve and mend the relationship
Style	asssertive	assertive
Skills	eye contact, clear and loud voice, avoid quarrels, convincing reasoning, sticking with interests and claims	eye contact, clear and loud voice expressing own emotions, understanding the needs and emotions of the partner, compromising
Success	goals achieved	relationship strengthened

Exercise: Levels of Communication

Learn the differences between the levels of communication with the following exercise. Start with the outer, more superficial level and move inward toward intimacy. Use the sentence/question examples as a guide.

Fifth Level: Clichés
"What's up?"
"Nice weather, isn't it?"
"How was your day?"

Fourth Level: Facts
"I heard about this on the news . . ."
"I read this chapter on communication and . . ."

Third Level: Ideas and Opinions
"My opinion about this exercise is . . ."
"I think the point is . . ."
"I realized that . . ."

Second Level: Emotions
"Since we have started to work more seriously on our relationship, I feel . . ."
"I feel you are close to me when . . ."
"I like you the most when . . ."

First Level: Intimate Communication
"I want you to know that . . ."
"My desire about you is that . . ."
"It is good to be with you when . . ."
"It is good to be with you because . . ."

{communication}

Toward, Away, and Against

Write a few sentences below. Imagine hearing these from your partner, and try to develop a "toward," an "away," and an "against" type of response.

1. **I'm so bored.**

    Toward:

    Away:

    Against:

2. **This stupid computer has crashed again!**

    Toward:

    Away:

    Against:

3. **You chose this one again? You know how much I hate this series!**

    Toward:

Away:

Against:

Passive, Assertive, and Aggressive

To understand the difference between passive, assertive, and aggressive answers better, write an answer for each type.

1. A husband has been waiting all day for the evening football game. Everyone was talking about it at work; it's a really big game. At home his wife informs him that evening that there is going to be the most anticipated episode of her favorite show and there is no way she is going to miss it because of a silly football game.

    Passive:

    Assertive:

    Aggressive:

2. You and your partner are going to the movies. Your partner seems to be dragging his or her feet, unable to get ready on time. This situation has repeated itself, and you feel it is time to express your disapproval:

{communication}

Passive:

_____

_____

Assertive:

_____

_____

Aggressive:

_____

_____

3. Your partner lent someone your favorite CD without consulting you. This is really bothering you, and you tell her/him your disappointment:

Passive:

_____

_____

Assertive:

_____

_____

Aggressive:

_____

_____

4. You had a heated debate with your partner. You reflect on it afterward and realize that you were mostly to blame. You want to make amends:

Passive:

_____

_____

Assertive:

_____

_____

Aggressive:

_____

_____

5. A husband meets with a neighbor's wife on the street and engages in a deep conversation about her husband's new job. His wife sees the conversation through the window. She does not know what the conversation is about, but gets a funny feeling and becomes jealous. She makes a scene when her husband gets home. Her husband says:

Passive:

_____

_____

Assertive:

_____

_____

Aggressive:

_____

---

[1] A. Bochmann, *Praxisbuch Ehevorbereitung*, p. 50.

[2] Bryan Craig, *Searching for Intimacy in Marriage* (Silver Spring, Md.: Ministerial Association, General Conference of Seventh-day Adventists, 2004), pp. 75-77. Craig's reference is from John Powell: *Why Am I Afraid to Tell You Who I Am?* (Argus Communications, 1960), pp. 50-56.

[3] John M. Gottman and Joan DeClaire, *The Relationship Cure* (New York: Three Rivers Press, 2001), pp. 26ff.

[4] *Ibid.*, p. 37.

[5] John M. Gottman, *Why Marriages Succeed or Fail* (New York: Simon & Schuster, 1994), pp. 56ff.

[6] Mihalec Gábor, *Áspiskígyók és palimadarak: a magabiztos kommunikáció kézikönyve* (Budapest: Athenaeum 2000 Könyvkiadó, 2004), p. 19.

[7] Olson, Olson-Sigg, and Larson, p. 43.

[8] Jürg Willi, *Koevolution: Die Kunst gemeinsamen Wachsens* (Reinbek bei Hamburg: Rowohlt, 1985), p. 143.

7

{ conflict resolution: }
stumbling blocks or stepping-stones

Icebreaker Questions:
- Try to recall your last successful quarrel. What made it a "successful" one?
- How did your parents work through their conflicts? What have you learned from them?
- What do you want your mate to do (or not to do) during conflicts?

Take a deep breath—a difficult subject is on the table. My friend and colleague, Robert Csizmadia, usually begins his premarital counseling with a question he learned from older colleagues: "Have you ever quarreled?"

The question usually surprises the couples, as they do not know what the "right" answer should be. Some couples force on themselves an idealistic view of their relationship, so they say that they love each other enough to have never fought. What do you think of such a response? In this case Robert usually advises the couple to postpone the wedding until just after the first real quarrel.

No marriage exists without conflict. The basic dynamics of marriage itself bring a range of tensions. Two persons, who have been independent, decide to spend the rest of their life together in the same space. So instead of making decisions on their own (what to do, how to spend time and money, and many other things), they now have to agree upon things, and this very process entails quarrels and disagreements. They made a decision to be together and stay together, to become "we," but that means giving up a lot that goes with being an independent "I."

We Work With Materials You Bring

Nobody gets married with an empty bag. It's like a potluck—everybody brings something: identity, habits, experiences, personal tastes, a value system. The big question is how the two individual bags fit together. David Mace,[1] in his previously mentioned classic book, classifies three groups of raw materials brought in by spouses:

1. Congruent Living Patterns. They are the habits and activities that both partners like. For example, they love Beethoven and tennis, and their favorite dish is spaghetti. Such areas will hardly cause a conflict and will bring joy in their marriage.

2. Complementary Living Patterns. This is a bit trickier. Such patterns include characteristics that differ but can still in some way complement each other. For example, one likes to drive, while the other one navigates. One prefers to iron and the other likes washing dishes. It takes time for a couple to sort out the complementary features and coordinate activities and tasks, but such patterns will eventually be valuable resources for the relationship.

3. Clashing Living Patterns. Here we find the hardest materials to deal with: characteristics that contradict and oppose each other. One likes to get up early, while the other could sleep until noon. One doesn't prefer sex, while the other is sexually overcharged. Some of these conflicts will eventually be resolved, but others refuse to change. As psychologist Dan Wile[2] puts it: "When choosing a partner for a long period of time . . . the choice will inevitably include some unsolvable problems you will have to live with for 10, 20, or 50 years."

Gottman adds that "marriage is good, if you manage to choose a problem you can cope with."

The key is how a couple will handle the diversity of their marriage. We cannot distinguish between happy and unhappy couples on the basis of their disagreements, *but rather by how they handle them.* Most experts concur on this crucial importance.

Bryan Craig writes that "current research clearly shows that the greatest obstacle to achieving intimacy and satisfaction in marriage is a couple's inability to handle successfully their conflicts and disagreements. It is not how much they love each other, how great their sex life is, or even how they deal with their money or discipline their kids that best predicts the quality of their relationship—it is the way they deal with their differences."[3]

Virginia Satir, a pioneer of family therapy, believed that individuals cannot be real or develop a truly human and zestful relationship until they have confronted and successfully handled their differentness.[4]

And finally, an honest confession from the pen of Gottman: "But I believe we grow in our relationships by reconciling our differences. That's how we become more loving people and truly experience the fruits of marriage."[5]

Are you sure you know the real issue you might be quarreling about? Sometimes it happens that the couple sitting in front of me starts an argument about a seemingly insignificant subject, and I get the feeling that there is something more going on than what they are disclosing. Beneath the surface, something entirely different is driving the conflict. We then spend the subsequent discussion on finding out the real reason. The following list presents some factors that often play into conflicts in marriage, but are rarely openly acknowledged.[6]

- ***The issue of power.*** It is a common motivation of the fights. Such quarrels are not about how to address real problems, but whose solution will be accepted, who has the last word, who can enforce his or her will over the other.

- ***The issue of love.*** Spouses need to feel safe and be sure that they are loved, that they are important to each other, and that each takes the needs of the other seriously. If they do not feel loved, frustration can easily turn into bitterness and blame.

- ***The issue of recognition and acceptance.*** If spouses receive praise from each other, they feel valued in the relationship. This helps prevent burnout of the relationship, and enables them to address problems more effectively. Rejection and fear of losing the other's respect put unnecessary strain on the relationship.

- ***The issue of commitment.*** The sense of security is critical in a marriage. If one party feels that the other may pack up and leave at any time, it will build anxiety and emotional barriers that make it impossible to deal with conflicts.

- ***The issue of integrity.*** Our words and our actions must be consistent with our values and inner thoughts. Few things undermine effective conflict management more than questioning each other's sincerity and motives.

As we can see from the list, the issue is usually not who would take the garbage out or who would mow the grass. That's only the tip of the iceberg. The real trouble is smoldering under the surface.

Conflict Management Styles

A number of marriage researchers list five conflict management styles, based on categories borrowed from business research. They develop along two important factors: one involves how the person pursues his or her own needs, and the other reflects how much attention the person is willing to give to his or her partner's needs. For simplicity's sake, researchers and counselors often associate the approaches with animals that demonstrate the dominant character of the style.

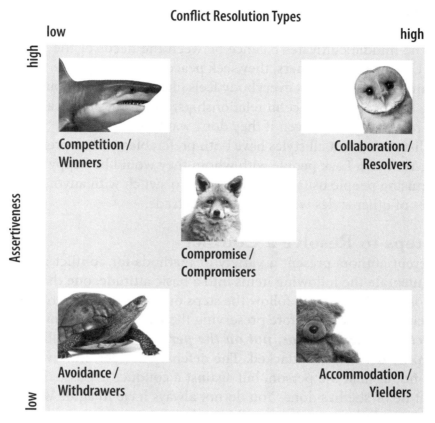

• **Competitive sharks.** Competitors pay attention to their own needs but do not care about the partner's interests or wishes. Such people tend to argue convincingly and act effectively, and their reasoning is compelling. But they achieve their goals by trampling over others, who will then feel lonely in their relationship and often that their conscience has been violated.

• **Accommodating teddy bears.** The bears are the opposites of sharks. They pay lots of attention to others but little to themselves. Their slogan is "As you wish!" Always ready for sacrifices, they are good in serving and giving and giving and giving. But they often feel martyred. They would do anything to keep from losing their mate's love.

• **Collaborative owls.** These types pay lots of attention to the needs of both their partners and their own. Preserving the relationship, peace, and effectiveness are all-important for this style. They do not get up from the negotiating table until they have achieved an acceptable solution. It can be very tiring to invest great energy in resolving *all* tensions. They tend to be idealistic, and because of their persistence they may seem pushy at times.

• **Avoiding turtles.** Turtles do not pay attention to the interest of themselves or of their partner—or even the relationship itself. In case of a conflict they will

{conflict resolution}

hide under their imaginary shell just like turtles. Sometimes they peek their heads out just to bite. Because they have time in their retreat to process events, they generally are not tense. However, it is hard to communicate with them during conflicts because they clam up and avoid the issues.

• ***Compromising foxes.*** Employing a cleverness illustrated by the fox, one type in the middle cultivates balance between the needs of the partner and of the self. Usually good listeners, they seek peace and respect others. They resolve most conflicts in a way that everybody feels like a winner. Although they generally have balanced and peaceful relationships, sometimes they can feel enslaved by their role and give in, even if they don't want to.

The list shows that all styles have both preferable and less preferable characteristics. Yet when I ask people with whom they would be happy to swap styles, compromising people usually do not prefer to switch with anyone, while representatives of other styles would be happy to trade.

The Steps to Resolve a Conflict

Different authors present a variety of methods for conflict resolution. But we can integrate the following items into a basic attitude, one that will be helpful in most conflicts. If you follow the steps outlined, any disagreement will get adequately discussed, therefore preserving the feelings of love and respect.

• ***Focus on the behavior, not on the person.*** Everyone will automatically stand on the defensive if attacked. The defense subsides, however, if the complaint is not against the person, but against a conduct. Disassociate the person and what he or she has done. You do not always have to agree with everything the other one does, but you can still love the person nonetheless.

• ***Say it respectfully.*** Respect has a central role in conflict resolution. Honoring each other will help keep you from crossing lines that would result in irreversible consequences. The disappearance of respect guarantees that the parties will move away from each other emotionally. One party may seek to emphasize his or her words by saying something shocking (name-calling, for example). In the subsequent quarrel it will be the starting point, so if the individual wants to gain momentum again, he or she must go further and use even stronger words that will be even more insulting. Can you guess how this will end? It is only a matter of time until the first slap. Respect helps prevent all that!

This is very important! Normally couples easily get carried away in the heat of an argument and tend to use words and gestures aimed to hurt. Take care, therefore, and always name exactly what you find disturbing in the other party's behavior. Avoid using words of ultimatum, such as "never" or "always." During a debate, deal with the present situation and don't seek revenge for past grievances.

• ***Practice positive communication.*** Remember what you have learned in "Communication—The Art of Listening." Keep in mind the five-to-one ratio and seek to express wishes, thoughts, and emotions with confidence (as opposed to the aggressive and passive methods).

• *Use humor.* A sense of humor disarms negative emotions. But be careful if you joke—do not make the other party the target of ridicule. That will backfire.

• *Take each other seriously.* Reassure each other in every debate that she or he is important and that her or his needs and interests will be considered. It is much easier to make a compromise with someone we know to be on our side, even if they do not agree with us. If you cannot agree, you can still show respect toward each other's feelings and opinions.

• *Your quarrels belong only to you.* Resist the temptation to share them with friends or your parents. Maybe you have resolved the differences long ago, but others who were needlessly involved will still be angered or frustrated toward your spouse.

The following table illustrates the differences between the constructive and destructive approach of the conflict management.[7]

	Constructive Approach	Destructive Approach
Issues	raises and clarifies current issues	brings up old issues
Feelings	expresses both positive and negative feelings	expresses only negative feelings
Information	gives complete and honest information	offers only select information
Focus	concentrates on the issue rather than the person	concentrates on the person rather than the issue
Blame	accepts mutual blame	blames the other person for the problem
Perception	focuses on similarities	focuses on differences
Change	facilitates change to prevent stagnation	minimizes change, increasing conflict
Outcome	recognizes both must win or both lose	a loss for the relationship
Intimacy	increases intimacy by resolving conflict	decreases intimacy by escalating conflict
Attitude	builds trust	creates suspicion

Four Horsemen of the Apocalypse

John M. Gottman[8] refers to a number of behavioral patterns that are predictable consequences of poor conflict management. Instead of resolving anything, they only deepen the conflict and create a greater distance between the couple. As Gottman says:

"If a conversation has a harsh startup, it is almost certain that it will return a negative result, even if the parties try to be 'kind' later on. The statistics speak for themselves: in the case of a quarrel lasting for 15 minutes, the outcome can be predicted with 96 percent accuracy based on the first 3 minutes!"[9]

The appearance of what I call the four horsemen of conflict unleashes deeper negative feelings at every stage and eventually isolates the partners, who will start to live in two separate worlds and evolve parallel lives. Let's look at them in their sequence.

1. Criticism: Negative content aimed at the character or personality of the partner, it can drive a wedge between two people who once were very close. It doesn't mean that nothing negative can be said in a marriage. Rather, we must distinguish between criticism and complaint. As opposed to criticism, complaint addresses only the specific action at which your spouse failed—according to your opinion—and not totally at the whole personality. In order for us to understand the critical difference between complaint and criticism, Gottman outlines them:

"Complaint: You should have told me earlier that you are too tired to make love. I'm really disappointed and I feel embarrassed. Criticism: "Why are you always so selfish? It was really nasty of you to lead me on. You should have told me earlier that you were too tired to make love."[10]

2. Contempt. The second rider is a direct result of the first. When a person has to swallow too much criticism, he or she begins to develop a growing contempt toward the other, and eventually it becomes visible as a facial expression and audible in words and intonation. Such contempt manifests itself in many ways: mockery, laughter, mimicry, hostile humor. Because it conveys hostility, contempt is always painful to the other. A typical example of contempt could be the following monologue:

"Just look at the difference in our vehicles and clothes. I think that says a lot of who we are and what we value. I mean, you tease me about washing my truck and you go and pay for somebody to wash your car. We are paying through the nose for your car, and you can't be bothered to wash it. I think that's outrageous. I think that is the most spoiled thing you do."[11]

3. Defensiveness. The first move of defensiveness is to give up fighting, and the parties then turn inward and start vindicating themselves. They no longer have a common cause or a desire to protect the relationship, but only to preserve their dignity and self-value. The defending parties don't admit that they have any part in the development of the conflict, but exempt themselves completely and blame the other.

4. Stonewalling. The most visible form of introversion is stonewalling. As the many insults build an impenetrable wall between the two partners, they start to pursue two separate lives, even if they live in the same home. The loud quarrels cease as they no longer try to convince each other anymore. Each one retreats into his or her personal, silent solitude. Physical symptoms often show that something is wrong at this point as the parties tend to develop insomnia, anxiety, or some other psychosis. Often the parallel lives will result in parallel relationships. At this stage the partners are much more inclined to get into an extramarital relationship. We see such a condition well illustrated by the monologue of Michelle Pfeiffer as Katie Jordan in the movie *The Story of Us*:

"I believe the loudest silences are those filled with everything that has been said. Said wrong . . . said 300 times. [. . .] Until fighting becomes the condition rather than the exception, and suddenly, without you even realizing it, it turns into the language of the relationship, and your only option is a silent retreat to mutual corners."[12]

The problem can be caught at an early stage and dealt with, however. If you feel that your statement was a criticism rather than a complaint, you have arrived at a point at which you have to turn back, or else you will end up in opposite corners.

The Sweet Taste of Forgiveness

We cannot proceed further in understanding the dynamics of marriage without knowing the final resolution of all differences: forgiveness. Every conflict causes internal tensions and changes: emotional fluctuations, loss of confidence, hurt, disappointment, humiliation. They must be processed in order to recommit and put the relationship on the path of growth. Forgiveness can be a lengthy process and often a difficult inner struggle. Everyone carries real or perceived grievances, and the happiness of the relationship depends on their ability to resolve such negative emotions with the other.

Few people realize that forgiveness does not mean doing a favor to the other party. Rather, it is part of our own *internal* growth. The process of forgiving forces us to sort out our thoughts and feelings concerning others.

But what motivates us to forgive? Because it looks good if we are the ones who initiate the release of tension and forgiveness? Reinhard Tausch, one of Europe's most influential psychotherapists, arrived at the following results based on his questionnaire-based research: "One of the major motivations for forgiveness is feeling compassionate toward the other person. We tend to forgive driven by an urge to do something good for the loved one to free the person from the burden of guilt. Second, we forgive to restore the deteriorated relationship, in order to continue life where it stopped before the conflict. Finally, we also forgive others to restore spiritual balance. To get rid of anger, rage, hatred, and the feeling of bitterness."[13]

As many might envision it: "Forgiveness removes the burden from me, and makes me happy again. It is me who feels better." "When I'm in conflict with someone, the strain on my heart upsets my peace of mind. And I think that the other party experiences the same. So by forgiving, I cause joy to the other and myself. Life blossoms again." "If I really manage to forgive someone, I feel that I've gotten rid of a huge burden. Hatred disappears at once."

Yes, such things should take place after each quarrel, but life is just not that simple. Many factors can limit or even prevent forgiveness.

1. Lack of skill and will. "I want to cause her pain for what she did to me." Or "There are things my husband just doesn't want to forget. He deeply hurt me, and I don't want to forgive him."

2. Revisiting the conflict frequently. Remembering again and again the triggering event will bring up negative feelings of humiliation and anger. "For days I could not think of anything else. I felt cheated, degraded, deceived, and deeply hurt." As long as we allow such feelings to linger, or even be cherished, we will not be free to forgive.

3. Domination. To crave power, or to wield it and be proud of the fact, will also hinder the inner processes that forgiveness needs. "If I were to forgive her, it would make me feel like getting on my knees in front of her. This would undermine my self-respect. I don't want her to feel superior." Many people postpone forgiveness because they want to keep the other one in control, and by doing that they feel they are protecting themselves from another episode of disappointment or hurt. In such cases it is important to clarify the standards of behavior that we need to respect after the act of forgiveness. Forgiveness cannot license the "perpetrator" to repeat the abuse!

4. Misconception about forgiveness. How we regard forgiveness very much influences our ability to grant it. For some, forgiveness is synonymous with weakness, permissiveness, or lack of self-confidence. "What kind of man am I if I just forgive and pretend as if nothing had happened? How will my friends see me? How could I look in the mirror?" Forgiveness does not mean that we dismissed or ignored the negative act in any way.

5. Low self-esteem. People who are dissatisfied with themselves and blame themselves for the mistake are more likely to be unable to forgive others as well. Some tend to overemphasize their own fault in the development of the conflict and thus cannot forgive themselves, so it becomes even harder to find a way to forgive the other. "I'm mad at myself for enduring his behavior for so long." This is particularly true of people who have depression or some other mental imbalance or disorder. Such a state of mind causes people to see themselves and the world very negatively, greatly curtailing the ability to forgive.

6. The offensive behavior continues. Often the person who has hurt us makes forgiveness difficult. It is very hard to forgive a person who continues his or her inconsiderate or abusive behavior and refuses to participate in the process necessary for resolving the problem. Many times people refuse to recognize that they also made mistakes that they need to deal with.

But there are also factors that can make it easier for us to forgive. Therefore,

> **29%** of the respondents stated that their belief had a significant influence in learning to forgive.

during a tension-laden period of time it is useful to direct our attention to them.

1. Self-examination. We can rethink our own judgments and position on the topic. In the study by Tausch that we previously cited, more than half of those surveyed stated that this step assisted in forgiving those who had caused hurt. "I'm trying to sort out my feelings. I challenge myself to discover why I should forgive. Is it worth it for me to keep the grudge? I rethink the issue and challenge my position." As a result, we are more able to evaluate our part in the conflict. The "You're wrong!" statement becomes self-reflective questions: "What have I contributed to the problem? What is my part in it, even if I didn't initiate it?"

2. To be aware of the disadvantages of holding grudges. "It helped me to forgive when I realized that a friendly atmosphere is better for both of us, because we had a positive relationship for so many years. It would be wrong to throw it all away by being unable to restart the friendship."

3. Empathy. Imagine yourself in the other person's situation. It can lead to a reevaluation of the stressful event. "I tried to put myself in my husband's thoughts and emotions. I imagined our quarrel from his point of view and thought about how his attributes determine my behavior. In the meantime I had to realize that considering how he was reacting, I would hardly have done otherwise." When you place yourself in the other person's mental state, it is much easier to see positive aspects. And if we reach a positive regard toward the other, it will have a direct effect in rekindling the relationship.

4. Religious beliefs and the ability to forgive. Religious people are in a better position when it comes to forgiveness, because they experience guilt and forgiveness as a reality. In Tausch's study 29 percent of the respondents stated that their belief had a significant influence in learning to forgive. "I'm working to do everything in the spirit of love. I have no right to judge."

It would be helpful for nonreligious people, those not influenced and motivated by the experience of faith, to meditate on a historical figure or a person they respect as an example of forgiveness. It is interesting in this regard to think of Jesus as a historical person, or of Viktor Frankl, the famous psychologist imprisoned in Auschwitz, where he lost his wife and his parents, yet could still forgive and didn't nurture hatred toward his captors and the murderers of his family.

5. Love toward the other. One of the most important factors of forgiveness in a marriage is that we are not dealing with a stranger who can exit our life at any time, but with the person to whom we are deeply attached emotionally, with whom we want to spend the rest of our days. If we look at our relationship from such a perspective, the potential loss will certainly dwarf most of the bickering.

Exercise: Potluck Materials

What kind of materials (issues) do you bring into your marriage? The following exercise can help identify them. List and group your characteristics in the provided spaces, then brainstorm together about how you could turn your clashing materials into an advantage in the relationship.

1. **Congruent Living Patterns:**
   _____
   _____

2. **Complementary Living Patterns:**
   _____
   _____

3. **Clashing Living Patterns:**
   _____
   _____

List ideas on how to use such possibly clashing living patterns for the advantage of the relationship:

_____
_____
_____
_____
_____
_____
_____
_____
_____
_____
_____
_____
_____
_____
_____
_____
_____

Ten Steps to Resolve a Conflict

Choose a less-traumatic conflict and try to find a solution with the help of the following 10 steps. If you find the exercise useful in smaller conflicts, you can use it to solve larger ones as well.

1. **Set a time and place for discussion. Reserve at least 30 minutes to talk.**

    Date: _____ Time: _____ Place: _____

2. **Choose a problem you want to tackle. List the topic or area of conflict.**

    _____
    _____

3. **List the ways each of you contributes to the problem. Try to be objective and resist laying blame.**

    Groom:

    _____
    _____

    Bride:

    _____
    _____

4. **List any unsuccessful past attempts to resolve the issue.**

    _____
    _____

5. **Brainstorm. Pool your new ideas and try to list at least five possible solutions to the problem. Do not judge or criticize any of the suggestions at this point.**

    _____
    _____

6. **Discuss and evaluate each of these possible solutions. Be as objective as possible. Talk about how useful and appropriate each suggestion feels.**

    _____

{conflict resolution}

7. Agree on one solution to try after you have exchanged your opinions and feelings. We are going to try the following solution:

   _____

   _____

8. Agree how you will each work toward this solution. Be as specific as possible.

   Groom:

   _____

   _____

   Bride:

   _____

   _____

9. Set up another meeting in a week to discuss your progress.

   Date: _____ Time: _____ Place: _____

10. Pay attention to each other during this process. If you notice your partner is making a positive contribution toward the solution, praise his/her effort.

---

[1] D. Mace, *Love and Anger in Marriage,* pp. 58-59.
[2] Quoted in J. M. Gottman and N. Silver, *Seven Principles for Making Marriage Work,* p. 143.
[3] B. Craig, *Searching for Intimacy,* p. 125.
[4] Virginia Satir, *Peoplemaking* (Souvenir Press, 1990), p. 138.
[5] J. M. Gottman, *Why Marriages Succeed or Fail,* p. 28.
[6] H. Markman, S. Stanley, and S. Blumberg, *Fighting for Your Marriage* (San Francisco: Jossey-Bass, 1994).
[7] D. H. Olson, A. Olson-Sigg, and P. J. Larson, *The Couple Checkup,* p. 71.
[8] Gottman and Silver, pp. 27-34.
[9] *Ibid.*, p. 26.
[10] *Ibid.*, p. 28.
[11] *Ibid.*, pp. 29, 30.
[12] *The Story of Us* (Universal, 1999).
[13] Reinhard Tausch, "Vergeben ein bedeutsamer seelischer Vorgang," *Pädagogisches Forum* 3 (1994): 125-136.

8

{ personality: }
mr. and mrs. mystery

Icebreaker Questions:
- What personality traits have you observed in each other that you greatly appreciate?
- What personality traits in your partner would you rather have altered?
- Do you think the similarities or opposites attract?

A not-so-bright young man decided he would not get married until he found the perfect woman. He imagined the woman of his dreams to be clever (but not smarter than he was), slim, pretty, precise, orderly (but not obsessively), a good housewife, and a good communicator (but not overly chatty). A few years later he met an old friend who asked him if he had found the perfect woman.

"I've met pretty, precise, smart, orderly women,

but have not found one with all the characteristics. I'm still looking for the one."

A few more years passed, and the now-not-so-young man once more encountered his old friend, who again inquired about the search results.

"I have found her!" was the answer. But with a sigh, he continued, "The only problem is that she is looking for the perfect man."

Humanity has been concerned about personalities for a long time. The ancient Greeks observed character traits and tried to group them into categories, eventually leading to the Hippocratic model. People still use it today. The father of medicine believed that the proportion of bodily fluids determines human personality, and that is why the Greek names of various bodily fluids became the terms used to define the four basic personalities: choleric, phlegmatic, melancholy, and sanguine. Modern researchers have proposed additional classifications.

Fritz Riemann[1] introduced a model based on anxiety that illustrates personalities as planets. Various forces influence a person, and the dominant power determines the personality. Some seem to rotate around themselves, as the earth does around its axis. This is the personality Riemann calls *schizoid*. Others always orbit around other people, like the earth does around the sun, and they tend toward a more depressed personality. Then he identified two more types analogous to centrifugal and centripetal forces: the obsessive and hysterical personalities.

In recent times a five-factor model of personality, the so-called Big Five, has conquered scientific circles (its scientific name is NEO FFI). But these theories represent only a few examples of the many models and extensive research that deal with personality. Once we have chosen the model that we favor, we can start playing a game: Which personality fits best? You can decide if opposites attract, or if similar ones draw each other in.

We face two major problems in the practical application of selecting a mate based on personality analysis. First, when seeking a life partner, we rarely do so by lining up the optimal candidates, making them fill out tests, and comparing test results against a rigorous interview session. In most cases we get to know someone, we fall in love, and we end up in a relationship. At this stage a test is no longer useful. It can help us decide only whether we want to *continue* the relationship. Second, our personality is something that generally sticks with us through all our life. In other words, certain aspects of it we will probably never be able to change. Thus the knowledge of personality models is helpful in understanding *how* personalities work, but will not help much in altering them.

Even if the knowledge of personality types has only a limited usefulness while selecting a mate, we can much better utilize it when planning a common life with the person we have already found. In this case the precise mapping of the potential mate's personality will help you understand why you react in a specific way in certain conditions, and why you relate to people as you do. Each personality type has strengths and challenges.

In the next few paragraphs I'll give an overview of the Riemann personality types. I picked this approach from the many theories available, because it is well organized and easy to understand. It also presents an explanation for behavior in a relationship. Maybe the names of the types are somewhat misleading, as we can easily associate them with mental illness, but belonging to a certain group does not mean abnormality. Remember, everyone finds themselves in one of the groups, even while mentally healthy.

1. The schizoid personality. As the earth rotates around its own axis, the schizoid personality types prefer to be centered on themselves all day—everything is about them. Unfortunately, however, they worry that rules, laws, or obligations will tie them down, narrowing their opportunities and limiting their personal quest for freedom. We can summarize the positive and negative characteristics of this personality in the following table:

Schizoid Personality	
Advantages	**Disadvantages**
accepts self; original, different from others; draws boundaries; independent personality, not partial; very good observer; hates flattery; has critical judgment without taking sides; directs own fate; realistic, lives without illusions; a genius working hard on his/her own; very precise in work; focuses on the issues rather than on persons	wants to be different from others; isolated and lonely; finds it hard to belong; often feels misunderstood; feels easily rejected; afraid of dependence; impersonal and cold; unsure in relationships; hard to talk to; afraid of emotions; frustrated between emotions and reason; when becoming distrustful, will paint a false picture of the world

The most fitting job for the schizoid personality is one in which the individual can gratify his or her passion for precision, in which they can benefit from their own excellent ability to observe, and in which, if possible, they will not have to cooperate with others. In general, schizoids become scientists, physicists, mathematicians, diagnostic psychologists, quality supervisors, engineers, librarians, technical supervisors, observers (using microscopes or telescopes), photographers, and inventors.

If in love, a schizoid feels distant and distrustful. It is very difficult for them to commit, and they will rather choose cohabitation than the deep involvement of a marriage. In the case of a schizoid man, the woman usually does the proposing. Even in a relationship he needs more autonomy and independence than the other types. He's more the man of logical considerations rather than a person of emotions. However, once committed, this type will stick to the decision, even if the atmosphere is somewhat icy at home.

2. The depressed personality. Such a person always needs someone to live around, just as the earth orbits the sun. Since other people are always the center of their attention and life, individuals with the depressed personality are afraid to stand on their own feet, because they fear isolation or abandonment. Their sense of security derives from being with others.

The personality structure includes many positive attributes, but it has many properties that make life difficult and that leave the person vulnerable. I summarize them in the table below:

Depressed Personality	
Advantages	**Disadvantages**
adaptive, selfless, sympathizing; good team member; idealist, patient, communicative, makes friends easily; has rich emotional life; modest, faithful, self-sacrificing, attentive, caring; trustworthy, careful	dependent on the opinions of others; afraid of loss and departing; undecided, hard to arrive at a decision; subservient, cannot defend interests; perfectionist; has a tendency to masochism and pessimism; can be easily offended; idealistic in an unrealistic way

The depressed personality—as a result of its good characteristics—is very good in nonprofit, service, or caring jobs. They are among the best teachers, nurses, counselors, social workers, and pastors.

When in relationships, the depressed personality is able to express love very well, giving all to their mates and sacrificing everything for them. They create a loving and warm atmosphere around themselves. A depressed personality wants to please their mate, so they attend to his or her every wish.

Since such a personality is very considerate toward loved ones, they will give wonderful gifts. As a result they find the most suitable and personal item for every occasion. If the partner feels blue, however, the depressive person is prone to guilt and self-blame. Because of unlimited self-giving, such persons are at risk in experiencing every marital conflict as incredibly painful, and they typically suffer greater emotional fractures (cheating, abandonment, etc.). It can cause them to fall into apathy.

3. The obsessive personality. Perhaps we can best illustrate this type by the analogy of gravity, a force pushing downward. For this person the most important aspects are predictability, security, and stability. The obsessive personality is anxious about change, insecurity, murky situations, potential risks, or vast amounts of freedom. We summarize both the good and challenging characteristics on page 77.

The perfect jobs for the obsessive types are clerk, lawyer, engineer, accountant, proofreader, statistician, programmer, custodian, inspector, judge, and chemist.

In a marriage the obsessive personality is dutiful, reliable, and uncondition-

Obsessive Personality	
Advantages	Disadvantages
dutiful, persistent, traditional; thrifty, honest, thrives for recognition, painstaking; trustworthy, fair, responsible; clean and tidy; morally sound, obedient, consistent	principles are more important than persons; hypocrite, bossy; becomes slave of duties; thinks in black-and-white categories; rigid, inflexible, self-complacent; fanatical, stingy, cruel, judgmental

ally loyal. They respect and regard marriage as an institution, and are deep and well founded in love. Uncomfortable with surprises or experimentation, they often become prosaic in showing love, or even downright boring. Because such personalities fear spontaneity, they can be very challenging for the partner. They love with the head rather than the heart, and regard excessive emotional displays with suspicion.

4. The hysterical personality. Analogous to the earth's centrifugal force, the hysterical personality always hovers just a few inches above the ground. Such individuals are quick to say yes to development, to change, to break with tradition, and to set new targets. However, they also fear any loss of freedom or of limitation by rules and principles. Their key characteristics appear below:

Hysterical Personality	
Advantages	Disadvantages
very flexible even in challenging situations; adaptive; popular with friends, thrives to be special; can encourage and motivate well; self-conscious and secure; full of energy, a leader type; knows what he/she wants; goal-oriented; optimist; can represent his/her needs, wishes	not persistent enough; scattered thought patterns, too spontaneous; hyperbolist; anxiety of loss of freedom, or of being tied up; can be easily influenced; has too high expectations

The best professional orientation is a varied, creative job. Many hysterical personalities will become excellent actors, researchers, inventors, artists, interior designers, editors, graphic designers, speakers, politicians, shop assistants, or salespersons.

In love the hysterical personality can really be flattering, and their enthusiasm captivates the partner. They are generous with gifts, their presence is always fun, and they will not make a fuss out of insignificant matters. In addition, they look for excitement, pleasure, and variety. Their house is always open for guests, and they love to host parties. However, the desire for change may drive them into extramarital adventures. Because they have high self-esteem they tend to subordinate the partner to their own goals. Not only do they fall in love easily, they will slip out of it just as quickly. Furthermore, they take it very hard if their partner is ill.

You may have already started to speculate into which group you belong. I would like to facilitate your decision by a thorough personality test found in the appendix. With its help, you can determine exactly the type to which you belong.

I should point out that all personality types are of equal value. No one is better than another, as each has its own strengths and challenges. All of them are necessary for a balanced human coexistence. Furthermore, no one is a "pure" personality type, so no one is 100 percent schizoid or entirely obsessive. We are all mixtures of several personality types, but usually one is dominant, and it tends to determine a person's behavior. Knowing the personality structure can be helpful in understanding ourselves and our partners, but we cannot use personality types as an excuse for getting away with something self-serving (for example, a married hysterical cannot blame his or her personality for infidelity).

Other Personality Traits That Affect a Marriage

Aside from personality structure and the more or less unchangeable personality type, marriage researchers have observed personality traits, properties, and abilities that are independent of the personality type and that we can change. Being aware of them and consciously cultivating them will be an invaluable help in achieving a balanced relationship.

> *"No one personality type is better than another, as each has its own strengths and challenges."*

Through his extensive research, David H. Olson proved that there are four personality traits (regardless of personality type) that essentially influence the quality of the relationship.[2]

1. Self-confidence. We can define it as the degree of trust in our own abilities that enables us to achieve a goal. Such skills and abilities help us cope with the various challenges of life. Self-confidence shows just how "OK" we are with ourselves. If the parties involved in a relationship have high self-confidence, they will have a greater chance of a successful marriage. Therefore an important goal is to increase self-confidence during marriage preparation for all types of couples, and also in family therapy or marriage enrichment training.

2. Assertiveness. Assertive people are able

to clearly communicate their wishes without being aggressive or violent, and without violating the rights of others. Possessed of a healthy self-awareness and a firmness that matches a particular situation, they feel that the expression of personal thoughts, feelings, and wishes is a personal right. Being aware of themselves, their communication centers on "I" messages instead of "you" messages. If both parties in a couple treat each other assertively, the level of intimacy between them will increase, as they are able to express their wishes freely, increasing the likelihood of getting what they want.

3. Avoidance. We can define avoidance as an inability or disinclination to address problems. People with a low rate of assertiveness and a high rate of passivity show the highest rates of avoidance. Inversely, persons with high assertiveness display low rates of the characteristic. A growing body of research shows that sweeping problems and conflicts under the rug seriously threatens the durability of a relationship. Therefore it's important that married couples address sensitive issues.

4. Partner dominance. Partner dominance measures a couple's level of perception of how controlling they feel toward each other (not the *actual* level, but the *perceived* level). It is important to see that behind this trait there might be more than meets the eye. First, just because one partner is perceived as the dominant doesn't mean that he or she actually is. For instance, even an assertive partner might seem too firm or pushy to an indecisive person. Second, for someone to be able to become dominant, there must be another who will submit to them.

Research has shown that the four personality traits interact closely with each other. Self-confidence and assertiveness form a mutually reinforcing positive cycle. In other words, if one grows in self-confidence, that person will automatically increase in assertiveness, and vice versa. Similarly, avoidance and partner dominance strengthen each other. The more someone sweeps problems under the rug, the greater an individual will perceive their partner as controlling. Last, positive features can also be inversely linked with negative ones. The higher a person's self-confidence and assertiveness, the lower the avoidance and partner dominance.

What kind of personality fits us the best? Which personality type captivates

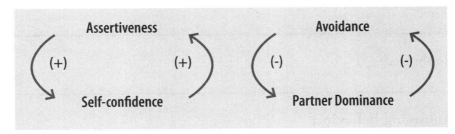

which? Do opposites or similarities attract each other better? That is difficult to answer. What is certain, though, is that the people who are happily married have high levels of self-confidence and assertiveness while maintaining low levels of avoidance and partner dominance. Furthermore, we can change or learn all these personality traits through conscious effort and attention. With the help of a PREPARE questionnaire you can find out if such personality traits are strengths or stumbling blocks in your relationship, and if they could be turned into stepping-stones with a little care and work.

Exercises: Reframing

List five of each other's characteristics that make you annoyed or frustrated. Then try to rephrase these characteristics in a way that would become a positive characterization (e.g., slow—thorough; stingy—thrifty; chatty—communicative; etc.).

The bride's list about the groom:

1. Annoying behavior:
   _____

   Rephrased:
   _____

2. Annoying behavior:
   _____

   Rephrased:
   _____

3. Annoying behavior:
   _____

   Rephrased:
   _____

4. Annoying behavior:
   _____

   Rephrased:
   _____

5. Annoying behavior:
   _____

   Rephrased:
   _____

The groom's list about the bride:

1. Annoying behavior:
   _____

   Rephrased:
   _____

2. Annoying behavior:
   _____

   Rephrased:
   _____

3. Annoying behavior:
   _____

   Rephrased:
   _____

4. Annoying behavior:
   _____

   Rephrased:
   _____

5. Annoying behavior:
   _____

   Rephrased:
   _____

Personality Test

Fill in the personality test in the appendix and discuss the following questions:

1. *What new things did I learn about myself with the help of the personality test?*
2. *What did I get to understand about your behavior, now that I know to which type of personality you belong?*
3. *What kind of challenges will my personality structure evoke in our marriage?*

{personality}

4. What kind of challenges will your personality structure evoke in our marriage?

5. How can we help each other cope with the challenges?

---

[1] Fritz Riemann, *Anxiety: Using Depth Psychology to Find a Balance in Your Life* (München: Ernst Reinhardt, 2008).

[2] David H. Olson, *PREPARE, PREPARE MK, ENRICH and MATE Facilitator's Guide,* Hungarian Edition (Szeged: Ketten Együtt Házassági Felkészítő és Tanácsadó Műhely, 2008), p. 52.

9

{ finances: }
gross dreams and net income

Icebreaker Questions:
- How did your parents deal with money? What kind of principles did you learn from them that you would like to follow in your own marriage? What might you like to do a different way?
- What kind of experience have you gathered so far about each other's spending habits in your relationship? Do these observations reassure you or worry you?
- If you received $500 that you could spend today, what would you buy with it? Who would be the one to decide how to use it?

"We don't talk about money," says a German proverb. And indeed they do not talk much about it. On one hand, they have enough; and on the other, the culture considers it a strictly private matter. It is an indiscretion if someone makes it a topic of conversation.

The case is different, however, in marriage preparation. Among the sources of marital conflict, finances occupy a prominent place. All people bring a value system from the family of origin, as well as any practices that they have themselves developed as adults. When two people connect their lives together in marriage, two different financial value systems also meet, and for the relationship to be as successful as possible, they have to be harmonized.

Many people believe that they are above the issues concerning money, most likely because it has had no impact on their family life. In my opinion, this is entirely impossible. On average, people spend 60 to 80 percent of their waking hours earning, spending, or thinking about money. It seems that money is a necessity, and it will also influence the marriage.

The Most Common Pitfalls

Most people have to figure out for themselves the best method of handling their money. It is not taught in school, and if we note society's general family spending patterns, they are also questionable. The table below lists certain money questions (based on the polling of 50,000 married couples)[1] that have been found especially influential on the happiness of a marriage:

Financial Issue	Percentage of Couples Having a Problem
1. I wish my partner would be more careful in spending money.	72
2. We have trouble saving money.	71
3. We have problems deciding what is important to purchase.	63
4. Major debts are a problem for us.	56
5. Credit card use has been a problem for us.	52

The findings by David Olson above also correspond with results of other studies, indicating that money (next to jealousy) is the cause of most marital fights. Every third couple believes that their partner is irresponsible with finances. Every fourth couple reports that the partner spends too much, and every fifth couple regularly fights over money.

Popular Myths Supported by Society

A number of social stereotypes (that culture has implanted in us without us noticing) for all practical purposes control our relationship with finances. We often just face the end result, when the consequences are already painful. The following list will address the three most common myths.[2]

- ***Possessions can make us happy.*** Society drills this myth into us from early childhood. Young people spend their pocket money right away, because the media insist that they can be cool only if they have the latest product. Saving has no value, because they will miss out on something good ("just now," "just for you," "limited edition," "while supplies last"). Those who grew accustomed to this way of thinking will surely be the pillars of consumer society as adults. Retail chains also lure buyers to fill the shopping cart with things they didn't originally intend to purchase. They rearrange shelves at regular intervals to force customers to go through the entire store just to find the item they came for. Naturally, during their search they will see several sales and new products.

A good defense is to go shopping with a list. You will then be more likely to buy only what you need and not what suddenly catches your eye. And remember: Never go into a grocery store while hungry! I tried it, and was shocked by the results. My $90 shopping list turned into $104 when I did the shopping hungry—I had a craving for everything I saw on the shelves.

- ***Debt is acceptable and unavoidable.*** The same way that we serve retail stores with the first myth, we do the same to the credit institutions with the second myth. Businesses lead us to believe that we need everything immediately. Even if we cannot afford it, we can *still* buy it now, and have time in the next few years (or decades) to pay for it. With some exaggeration, one could say that today's citizens buy, with money that is not theirs, stuff that they do not need, just to make people whom they do not like jealous.

Does this sound right to you? Do we have to buy this idea? Then do not allow commercials to take advantage of you! Credit institutions do not lend you money to help you—they lend because it's profitable for them. And if this sounds too strong, you should think about how high the interest rates are when the bank lends you money (bank loan), and how much interest the bank gives *you* for using *your* money (savings account). Occasionally a tenfold difference may exist between the two, even though the principle is the same: Someone is using someone else's money, for which the user of the money pays a fee (interest).

The recent economic crisis has shown how vulnerable we are in this area. Families lived with loans and big mortgages, and with the sudden increase of interest and the drop in income they became bankrupt. Many people lost their homes, while others had to take extra jobs, leaving little time for their families. Oftentimes such couples didn't calculate the risk of spending less time in cultivating their marriage, so they gradually became estranged from each other and sometimes ended up divorced.

Irresponsible use of credit cards causes the same kind of problems. Credit cards make it possible to have significant overdrafts on several credit accounts from different credit institutions. As a result, many have accumulated debts that will take 20 to 25 years to repay.

• ***A little bit more money will solve all our problems.*** An idea connected to the previous two, it illustrates the change that took place between the older and the present generations. "More" has become a slogan that covers all areas of life. We work more, and as we earn more, we spend more, using up more nonrenewable energy sources, accumulating more debt, and producing more garbage than any other generation in history.

So how do we get out of this mess? Good money management does not depend primarily on the amount of money. A larger income will not help the person who cannot balance the budget on little income. If the personal financial values and spending habits do not change, more money will only increase the demands. And it doesn't matter how large the income side of the budget is—it won't be enough, because expenses will also increase. Have you noticed that the wealthiest people also have the largest debts, and they can produce the most spectacular bankruptcies?

Who Makes the Decisions?

As we will observe in chapter 14 ("Roles and Relationships—Housekeeping in Style"), the best chance for a balanced, happy marriage exists when both parties feel equal in the relationship. This works in the realm of finances as well, so financial decisions are best made together. The marriage is a total economic community and is not governed by the same rules that regulate, for example, business life. It should not be that whoever earns more money has the right to make the decisions. Marriage is the community of two grown-up, equal persons, not a business enterprise. One partner may earn more, but the other partner may handle money better. And even considering those separate strengths, money decisions must involve mutual agreement.

Household Budget

Working out finances is an essential part of marriage preparation. Therefore, before you even start your life together you have to prepare your future household budget. On page 90 is a simple table in which you list all incomes and all expenses. It sounds banal, and maybe you think you have it figured out in your mind, but that is not enough. Believe me, it is quite different when detailed in hard numbers. The table will help you see your situation in black and white. Some items in the budget might sound a bit strange, so let's look at them a little closer:

• ***Savings.*** No financial unit can function smoothly without sufficient financial reserves. Marriage and family are no exceptions (that, however, does not contradict the fact that marriage is not a business venture). Unforeseen events can happen at any time, and the family will urgently need some cash (sickness, loss of job, etc.). Financial experts advise that the family should have a minimum reserve of three months' worth, an amount that will cover *all* living expenses for that period.

Aside from this, there are always financial goals worth consciously saving toward. And it is also important to invest in long-term savings, such as a retirement fund. And be wary, from time to time the temptation will arise to draw from your long-term fund(s). It is best, then, to regard them as nonexistent, or at least separate from your regular budget.

• **Marriage enrichment.** Into this category belongs every expense that you spend on your relationship: marriage books, enrichment seminars, a romantic weekend, etc. It will enable you not only to achieve your short-term goals but also a metagoal: Every month it will remind you that marriage needs care, attention, and nurture. If you invest money in something, you will also appreciate it more.

• **Donations.** You might find this budget item odd, but it is an important contribution to psychological well-being, child-rearing, and spirituality. To have money is to exercise responsibility. Those less fortunate might need your help. Do not think only of big things, as sometimes a gesture means more to a person in a hopeless situation than the fixed value of a donation. And I assure you that if you give to others, you will not necessarily have less. The old biblical wisdom is still true today:

"One person gives freely, yet gains even more; another withholds unduly, but comes to poverty. A generous person will prosper; whoever refreshes others will be refreshed" (Prov. 11:24, 25, NIV).

Conscious and regular giving will then convey an important ethical value to children, too.

Management Advice[3]

It is of little use if only one member of the family saves. The entire family should practice it, because only then will everyone pull the same end of the rope. Here are some ways to save together:

- Avoid wasting energy! Plan your car route so that with one trip you can accomplish several tasks.
- Don't leave the lights on when you leave a room.
- Do not turn on the heat when no one is at home.
- Don't leave electronic devices (computers, stereos, TV, DVD player, home theater, etc.) in standby mode. It may sound banal, but consider that in every country several power plants are working just to produce the necessary power to keep up with devices in standby mode.
- In case of larger investments (house, car, land, furniture, expensive equipment) you should solicit several independent bids so you can make the best possible decision. When you have all the requested information, sit down together so that every family member will be able to discuss the pros and cons. Examine what kind of impact the investment will have on

your future financial situation (e.g., how much it will cost to maintain, how much extra burden it will be on the family, etc.), and how it will affect the relationship between family members. Do not include in your decision how the new purchase will impress neighbors or coworkers.

- Be very critical toward limited-time offers. The louder they trumpet about something, the more persuasive the tactic behind an ad, or the more they write about the product's advantages, the more suspicious you should treat the matter. All products can be useful, but they are most useful to those who sell them!
- Look beyond the price of a product to its actual quality. It is a principle I have personally experienced recently with athletic shoes. For years I had been using a name-brand pair. After a while they wore out and I decided to go for a cheaper, no-name product. The result: In one year I used up three pairs of athletic shoes. Then I set for myself the following principle: "I'm not rich enough to afford cheap goods."
- Look for sales in things you already need. If you don't own the right loyalty or discount card, look for friends who do have it and ask them to buy the chosen item for you (with you then repaying them). In case of bigger purchases (washing machine, computer, refrigerator, etc.) the amount of the savings can be considerable.
- Get used to doing things differently than what everyone else does! Whenever it is possible, fight peer pressure. For example, try to take vacations at a different time than everyone else does, because most people take vacations at the most expensive time of year.
- Avoid investing in stocks or securities if you are not knowledgeable in international and domestic economics, or if you do not know all the rules of the stock market. Should you wish to invest in this manner anyway, pick a trustworthy investment company to do the job for you. But take into account that they have their own interests. In finances it is usually better to trust your own judgment and not to lean solely on an investment adviser's persuasion.
- Always read the fine print before signing a loan or a contract! The substance is always in the details. The drafter of the contract wants to compress into this part the obligations that they would rather conceal, but are legally required to list—and later on they can use it in litigation.
- You should sign a receipt of payment only after you receive the money and count it. Do not sign any contract, receipt, or even a sheet of paper that is blank.
- Do not bet everything on one card! Your savings are more secure divided into several funds and kept at more than one institution. Economic experts call this the centipede principle, because if the centipede loses a leg, it still has 99 to keep using.
- Beware of offers and bids that "seek only your benefit." In most cases the

bidder wants to give you the impression that they know your interests better than you do. Never forget: It is your hard-earned money and your decision.
- If you are keeping a bigger sum in the bank for a bigger expense, do not leave it in your checking account. Such accounts usually have interest rates lower than inflation, so such "savings" are practically losses. Choose a savings plan with a higher interest rate or an investment plan with fixed interest.
- When shopping for insurance, get several quotes for the same insurance package. Thoroughly examine what kind of services the insurance companies include in their packages and at what cost. Google that information and ask your acquaintances about their experiences with different companies. Aside from the insurance fees and services, it is also very important how fast, client-friendly, or circumstantial and bureaucratic an insurance company is when investigating a claim or paying for a damage. Remember that insurances include only the services listed in the contract. Forget all verbal communication with the agent. If you make a claim, only the contract matters.
- At least every four to five years, look through your insurance options to make sure they are still the most appropriate, and whether they are still valid for any changed circumstances. For example, insurance for sports accidents, which you took out in your 20s, might not be necessary in your 40s.
- If you want to save money but you don't have any extra income, you can still get started. Put aside a small part of your salary every month. For many families the 10 percent principle works. They consistently lay aside 10 percent of every source of income. Being fairly low in the family's budget, it will not cause a shortage, while at the same time it is significant enough in the long term and can grow into a surprising sum.

Exercise: Household Budget

Work out your shared household budget, following the plan on page 90. If you have any extra incomes or expenses not on the list, please include them as well. Aim for a total balance of incomes and expenses.

Discussion Points for the Budget Exercise:

1. Is your income larger than (or equal to) your expenses?

2. If you have a deficit, what would you need to change in order to achieve financial balance?

3. How much money will you save, even if you have a small income? Make an agreement!

{finances}

Budget		
Monthly Net Income	**Amount**	
Husband	$	
Wife	$	
Total Income	$	
Contributions	**Amount**	
Tithe	$	
Donations	$	
Monthly Expenses	**Amount**	
Housing		
Rent/mortgage	$	
Home maintenance	$	
Household expenses	$	
Utilities		
Telephone/Internet	$	
Gas/electricity	$	
Water/sewer	$	
Food		
Food at home	$	
Restaurant/cafeteria	$	
Children		
School/day care	$	
Pocket money	$	
Personal		
Hygiene/beauty	$	
Clothing	$	
Entertainment	$	
Transport		
Fuel	$	
Car services	$	
Car loan	$	
Other (bus/train)	$	
Other Expenses		
Insurances	$	
Taxes	$	
Medical	$	
Other expense	$	
Total Expenses	$	
Surplus or Deficit	$	

> The marriage is a total economic community and is not governed by the same rules that regulate, for example, business life.

Important Questions to Ask Yourself in Order to Avoid an Impulse Purchase[4]

If you want to buy something you didn't plan to purchase, quickly think through the following questions and decide based on your "yes" answers.

1. Do I really need it?
2. Is the price fair?
3. Is this the right time to buy it?
4. Am I sure that I cannot substitute something else?
5. Am I sure that it doesn't have any disadvantages?
6. If the price is too high, am I just seeking to satisfy an internal need?
7. Did I collect sufficient information about the item?
8. If it is a discounted product, how new is the model?
9. If the product claims to be discounted, is the original price the real and fair price?
10. Do you know if the seller is trustworthy?
11. Does the seller offer joint services (e.g., warranty, spare parts, etc.)?

Base your decisions on the YES answers:
9-11: Buy it.
6-8: Carefully consider the purchase.
0-5: Do not buy it.

---

[1] D. H. Olson, A. Olson-Sigg, and P. J. Larson, *The Couple Checkup*, p. 85.

[2] Dick Towner and John Tofilon, *Good Sense Budget Course Participant's Guide* (Grand Rapids: Zondervan), pp. 18ff.

[3] Compare Ernst A. Swietly, "Die schlechte Nachricht: Das Leben wird teurer. Die gute Nachricht: Dagegen läßt sich etwas tun—Die Devise heißt sparen," www.familienhandbuch.de.

[4] Bryan Craig, *Beginnings: A Pre-Marital Counselling Resource for Pastors* (Sydney: Adventist Institute of Family Relations, 2002), p. 158.

10

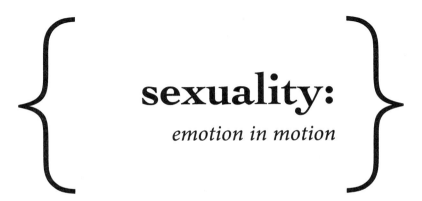

sexuality:
emotion in motion

Icebreaker Questions:
- What role does sexuality play in your relationship?
- In your opinion, how does premarital sexuality affect the relationship and the sexuality later in marriage?
- Are you satisfied with the degree of openness in your talk about sex? Rate it between 1 and 10.
- What helps you talk about the subject and what hinders you?

Marital research has shown that hardly any other area makes such a difference between happy and unhappy couples than sexuality. We can view sexual intimacy as the emotional barometer of a marriage. A good sexual relationship shows that the couple is emotionally in a good state and that they are satisfied with other aspects of their relationship. The following table will summarize the areas in which the difference is the greatest between the happy and unhappy couples.[1]

Sexuality Issue	Percentage in Agreement	
	Happy Couples	Unhappy Couples
1. I am completely satisfied with the affection I receive from my partner.	68	17
2. Our sexual relationship is satisfying and fulfilling.	76	28
3. My partner does not use or refuse sex in an unfair way.	82	36
4. I have no concerns that my partner may not be interested in me sexually.	84	40
5. I do not worry that my partner may consider an affair.	86	45

Secrets of Good Sexuality

An old university classmate of mine, Ralf Näther, examined people who are the most satisfied with their sexual relationship by interviewing 1,000 persons. According to his findings, the people most content with their sex life were those who: (1) have never been unfaithful, (2) have sex two to three times a week, and (3) talk openly about sexuality and explore novelties in a mutually accepted framework.

On the other hand, those who had the worst satisfaction scores were (1) unfaithful, (2) rarely had sex, and (3) refused any kind of variation from the "usual" way of making love.[2] Näther's research also proved that it is worth putting aside personal experiences, stereotypes, and taboos, and just examining the issues of sexuality openly.

What Is Normal?

Today's society accepts many things as "normal." However, that does not mean that you both have to regard every single sexual practice as "normal." Talk to each other about different sexual techniques and methods and shape your common view, considering your relationship, taste, health, your beliefs about morality, and what both of you label as "normal." To help you along, I'll share some useful and widely accepted guidelines. I believe they mark the general boundaries of normality:

- If it doesn't threaten any of the parties' physical or emotional health.
- If I participate because I want to, and because I want to cause joy for myself as well as my partner.

- If it doesn't include any coercion, and either of the parties can say no at any time.
- If I do it to express love toward my partner and not just use her or him.

Men Are Different. Women Are Too[3]

Each sexual relationship will have its troubles. Those difficulties usually involve the basic differences between men and women. Men tend to separate sex and relationship. Thus if a man is angry at his wife because of her long working hours, it doesn't make him abstain from sex at the end of the day. Women, however, tend to look at sex from a relational point of view. If the husband forgets to buy milk on the way home, as his wife asked him to, then she might lose her sexual appetite for the night. Sexual togetherness has different phases. Knowing them will help the couple fully enjoy this part of their relationship.

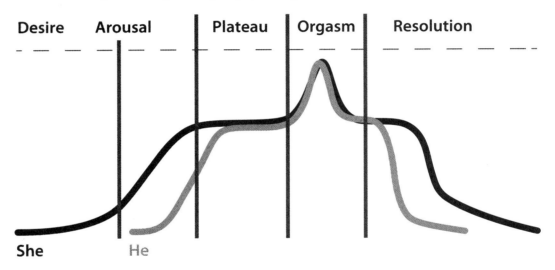

- *Arousal phase.* As the table shows, men and women experience it in significantly different ways. Men are aroused primarily by visual impulses, after which they are ready for sex. But for women, much more important are touching, stroking, and endearing words, because they create thoughts. Sexual excitement also has visible signs: men get an erection, women get wet (lubrication of vagina) and experience swelling of the nipples.
- *Plateau phase.* We use the word "plateau" to refer to a level, period, or condition of stability, so this phase has the same characteristics. The physiological processes that started in the previous phase are still active, and here they produce a continuous and pleasurable feeling. It is worth observing that the phase lasts much longer in women than in men. As a result, women need longer foreplay. If a couple ignores it, it is possible that the man will finish too soon and the woman will not be able to reach her orgasm.
- *Orgasm.* Orgasm is a wonderful experience, accompanied by the constrictions of abdominal muscles up to five to eight times. For men, friction and motion trigger this stage. For women, however, the process is much more complex.

While the aforementioned physical movements are important, intimacy and romantic and emotional arousal play bigger roles.

- ***Resolution phase.*** Relaxation follows the orgasm, which occurs faster in men, and is accompanied by a period when they cannot again be stimulated. The excitement level reduces much more slowly in women.

Sexuality in the Media

Sex is all around us. We run into it when we pay in the convenience stores as erotic magazines stare at us—and their cover pages already show a lot. We meet sexuality even in advertisements intended for children. Marketing seems to focus on three ways to sell a product: children, puppies, and sex. During prime broadcast hours we will observe who, when, where, how, and how often. Morning radio shows are especially explicit, flippantly sprinkled with sexual comments and conversations. Schoolkids can reach any offensive porn Web site within three clicks or less. I could go on. We have an informational overflow of sexuality. What is surprising, however, is that such messages rarely involve affection, responsibility, loyalty, commitment, or marriage. They give a very deformed picture of sexuality, one that has a strong influence on us. The more often we stumble into this distorted presentation of sexuality in seemingly harmless places, the less we will be sensitive to its offensiveness. Such deformed sexuality culminates in pornography. The problem with pornography is that it looks at human beings as objects, whose main function is to give sexual pleasure. Ultimately, watching pornography and its related sexual practices with or without a partner(s) can cause serious emotional addictions difficult to break.

Stephen and Alex Kendrick, the duo behind the great marriage movie *Fireproof,* comment in their book *The Love Dare:* "Watch out for parasites. A parasite is anything that latches on to you or your partner and sucks the life out of your marriage. They're usually in the form of addictions, like gambling, drugs, or pornography. They promise pleasure but grow like a disease and consume more of your thoughts, time, and money. They steal away your loyalty and heart from those you love. Marriages rarely survive if parasites are present. If you love your spouse, you must destroy any addiction that has your heart. If you don't, it will destroy you."[4]

Sex Before Marriage

What is your opinion about sexual activity before marriage? For many, such a question doesn't even cross their mind—they just have sex as often as they can. Others want to wait until they establish a sound relationship. Still others want to save the first major event for the wedding night, because they belong to a religious community. Whichever group you might be in, you should consider a number of facts about sex before marriage.

The first important one is the connection between sexuality and communication. Several researchers agree that during the introductory period of a relationship the couple will experience an intense development of interpersonal communication. The more they are together, the more intimately and more deeply they can talk to each other. They discuss a lot and do so intensively. During this time they will learn how to handle their conflicts. Interestingly, however, after the first sexual experience such intensive growth stops. Sex will take the place of speaking. In the light of this, it is best if sexual activity comes as late as possible, giving more time for the couple to develop interpersonal skills (communication, conflict management, accepting each other's personalities, etc.). I have seen in many couples how they will then continue to communicate with each other on the same level at which they got stuck at the time of their first sexual experience.

Sexual activity before marriage often means experience with multiple partners, which has a disturbing effect on marriage. When couples attending counseling complain about not being in sync sexually, often behind the problem is the fact that they compare their actual partner with someone from their past. And sometimes the previous partner had a greater sexual appetite or had more experience, etc. A couple's sexual relationship is an element of their oneness, something that they have to develop. Under normal circumstances they slowly learn to harmonize with each other. Step by step they discover each other's bodies, desires, and sexual responses. But it can be very disturbing—and even humiliating—when someone has to compete with a previous partner.

It is vital that couples engage in activities that do not involve sex, because it allows them to develop their relational skills. If they learn them before marriage, they will retain these skills, and the couple will find them very useful at some point in their marriage. As one of my male clients told me, "After my wife gave birth her episiotomy got inflamed. Therefore we could not make love for a long time. Later she got the baby blues, so she did not want to have sex at all. If we hadn't learned before marriage to show each other love without sex, I am not sure if I could have survived this period."

What Should We Do About Jealousy?

I mentioned before that being unfaithful affects sexual satisfaction. And if there develops even a suspicion of unfaithfulness, we face the next issue, which definitely has to be dealt with in connection to sexuality: jealousy. There exist many views and theories about jealousy, just as there do about sexuality. Let's look at two of them: 1. Jealousy is a sign of distrust and thus a burden to the relationship. 2. Jealousy is a sign of love, and protects the relationship against outside dangers.

Both definitions have some truth, and thus much depends on how you define jealousy. Jealousy has several types:

1. Pathological jealousy. If one party reacts often and heatedly to events that others term normal and usual, we refer to it as pathological jealousy. Often threats of violence toward the partner or toward the supposed rival will accompany it. In most cases this is not a relationship problem, but something resulting from a personality disorder of the jealous party. In this case it is worth seeking external help, as in psychotherapeutic or psychiatric treatment.

2. "Normal" jealousy. In these situations one party displays jealousy, but it is based on reality. Therefore, in order to protect the relationship, the partners need to take seriously the events that brought about jealousy. We can speak of normal jealousy when one party was unfaithful but decided to save the relationship. Such a couple has to rebuild trust, and during this time any behavior that brings about more jealousy is harmful.

A similar situation can occur with couples when one party desires a freedom that the other cannot tolerate. It may not even involve big things. In life we experience many situations in which the "guilty" party did not intend to do anything wrong, but the other still feels hurt. What happens if:
- The wife has an intense conversation with a man at a party?
- The husband has a female colleague with whom he shares intimate topics?
- The wife goes with her friends to a restaurant and the group includes men?
- The husband kisses, on the cheek, a woman who is unknown to the wife?

The partners' answers to these questions can be different, depending on what they regard as infidelity. Because disloyalty does not start in the bedroom of a stranger, every couple needs to define what they regard as faithfulness, and which behaviors cause insecurity.

Unfaithfulness on Different Levels

Remember the Sternberg triangle? In chapter 5—"The Goal of Marriage: 1+1=1"—we got to know three aspects of love: passion, intimacy, and commitment. When determining unfaithfulness, we may find it helpful to elaborate on these three aspects of love, because unfaithfulness can happen in all three. Most obvious is the infidelity that happens in the area of intimacy. It is what movies and TV series most frequently portray, and most wives talk about in counseling:

"My husband has somebody." At the same time, someone can be unfaithful on the field of passion. Maybe nothing happens sexually between the spouse and the third person, but the enthusiasm that the "unfaithful" party shows toward the third party can be very painful for the partner. Finally, a person can be unfaithful in such a way that he or she will not keep the commitment to the partner as promised in the vows. Such a letting down of the spouse can happen both in the small things of everyday life and in the greater issues.

Types of Contraception

To conclude the chapter, we must address the subject of contraception. Before the wedding, learn about the different methods available and choose one together that you think is most acceptable. Use the table on page 98 for some basic information.[5]

Finally, we will briefly consider abortion. Abortion is *not* a method of birth control. Nevertheless, in most Western countries it is a legal procedure. On a global level the number of abortions per year runs into the millions. Since it is a surgical procedure, it can cause physiological side effects, which may affect the chance for a later pregnancy. It also has an impact on the emotional and psychological well-being of the couple, and they might carry the wounds for decades. Besides, an abortion initiated for convenience (not because of health reasons) raises questions on moral grounds.

	Effects	Reliability and efficacy	Instruction	Possible side effects, complications	Preferences
Pill	hormonal method to prevent eggs from being released from the ovaries; thickens cervical mucus to prevent sperm from entering the uterus, and thins the lining of the uterus to prevent implantation.	if used correctly, 99.7 percent	daily 1 pill for 3 weeks or 28 days as ordered	evening nausea, possible weight gain, increased risk of deep-vein thrombosis (DVT) or clotting, though mostly in smokers	very safe, if user is organized enough to take consistently
Loop or strings (IUD)	the copper stops the sperm from making it through the vagina and uterus to reach the egg, thus preventing fertilization	97 percent, if regularly checked	inserted by a doctor; needs regular checkups	cramps, pelvic inflammatory disease, painful and heavy periods, backaches and headaches	gives constant protection
Diaphragm with jelly or cream	works as a mechanical block	very trustworthy, if used correctly	needs to be inserted in the vagina before the sexual act	can feel uncomfortable, but won't cause any other problems	if used correctly, will not cause any problems
Condom	works as a mechanical block	98 percent, if used correctly	needs to be placed over the penis before the sexual act	can feel uncomfortable, but won't cause any other problems	if used correctly, will not cause any problems

Exercise: I feel that you love me when you . . .

Complete the following sentences and discuss ways to make your sexual life more exciting.

1. I feel that you love me when you . . .

2. I feel that you are sexually attracted to me when you . . .

3. I feel your affection when you . . .

4. I get aroused when you . . .

Defining Faithfulness

Using your own values, define the meaning of faithfulness. Then suggest behaviors that contradict your definition of faithfulness. Fill out the form separately, discuss your opinions, and formulate a shared statement of what faithfulness involves.

Complete the following sentences:

According to the husband, unfaithfulness is: _____

_____

According to the wife, unfaithfulness is: _____

_____

According to the husband, faithfulness is: _____

_____

According to the wife, faithfulness is: _____

_____

The mutual understanding of faithfulness: _____

_____

The mutual understanding of unfaithfulness: _____

_____

[1] D. H. Olson, A. Olson-Sigg, and P. J. Larson, *The Couple Checkup*, p. 106.
[2] Andreas Bochmann and Ralf Näther, *Sexualität bei Christen: Wie sie ihre Sexualität leben und was sie dabei beeinflusst* (Giessen, Basel: Brunnen, 2002), pp. 127, 128.
[3] In this book I describe a healthy sexuality; however, couples can experience difficulties that might need professional help. I wrote about sexual problems in my book: *Istenadta szex* (*God-given Sex*; Budapest: Élet és Egészség Könyvkiadó, 2004).
[4] Stephen and Alex Kendrick, *The Love Dare* (Nashville: B&H Publishing Group, 2008), p. 112.
[5] B. Craig, *Beginnings*, p. 115. The chart was adapted by Gáspár Róbert Habil.

11

{ **parenting:** *the making of mom and dad* }

Icebreaker Questions:
- What makes a couple good parents?
- How does it make you feel that one day you might become a parent? What are the joys and fears associated with it?
- How will your relationship change once you become parents?

Every couple should discuss three important questions about children before the wedding: when, how many, and how? In this chapter I will try to assist you in answering them.

When?
Marriage will change several areas of your relationship. Life together brings up a number of issues that

require the development of mutually accepted rules and new habits, and you will need to tune in to each other for nearly 24 hours a day. Such things take time, so it is not good to add another task to deal with too soon after the wedding—namely, parenting. Unless you have special circumstances that justify having children right away, it is worth it to wait a few years. You can determine the ideal time based on important requirements and circumstances, but without necessarily setting a specific time or date.[1]

- ***You are living in a happy and stable marriage.*** Start the adventure of parenthood if you really enjoy your marriage. If you are uncertain in your relationship, postpone having children, because procreation is *not* a conflict management technique. Many have tried to draw their mate closer with a child, but most of them end up divorced. Because raising children means an added stress on the marriage, it can succeed only within a stable relationship.
- ***You are financially balanced.*** Taking care of children is expensive, so you need to have a certain level of financial stability. When preparing your budget, consider that one of you might not have an income (or maybe a decreased one) for a certain period of time. Build up savings for unexpected events!
- ***There is no external pressure.*** Do not have the children solely to make someone else happy! It is your life and your choice, and make it only if both of you really want it.
- ***You both feel that the right time has come.*** Sometimes the pressure does not come from the outside, but from one of the spouses. Since both of you will have equally important roles to play in raising your child, make it a joint decision!
- ***You are prepared for a major change in your marriage.*** The parental role is for a lifetime—there is no turning back. Although much of the changes are positive, parenting also has very stressful aspects. Discuss your fears and concerns honestly with each other.

How Many?

Many factors will affect the number of children you may desire.

- ***Family patterns.*** People from large families want many children themselves, and those who grew up as an only child are more inclined to have one child and provide for him or her in abundance. If one partner comes from a large family with lots of siblings while the other is an only child, there may have to be some negotiation.
- ***Medical or biological status.*** Some cannot have children because of age, complications during a previous delivery, or other medical reasons.
- ***Oops!*** Not every childbirth may be planned. A couple should be prepared to raise more children than intended in case of inadequate birth control.
- ***Financial abilities.*** As mentioned above, having children has financial implications. Therefore, common sense demands that you consider how many you can responsibly take care of within your income.

- **Values and worldview.** Various personal, moral, and religious values can also influence your preferred number of children. For example, some religious communities do not accept contraception on moral grounds, and its families have many more children than others.

The Effects of Children on a Marriage

The birth of a child fundamentally changes the lives of the parents, and it will show not only in the interior decoration of the home but also in the couple's relationship with each other and with their environment.[2]

- **The change in the relationship with the parents.** Many parents will start to treat their children as adults when the children themselves become parents. As long as a couple does not have children, their parents are still the focus of their extended family. They will spend the holidays with them, and family gatherings with other siblings will most likely be hosted at their home. With the birth of the first child, however, the new family focus will shift inward. From that time on, the parents are coming to visit. And from that point on, the new grandparents will regard the couple's relationship as their internal, private matter.

- **The change in social relations.** People without children can live a fairly separated life from their environment (except when paying bills, shopping, or going out). The child, however, just may facilitate relationships with neighbors who will be interested in the baby and will give "free advice" on child-rearing from time to time. Then, beginning with kindergarten and grade school, they will become part of a whole system of institutions.

- **Parents often find new friends.** The birth of a child will cause parents instinctively to seek the company of other parents, and they will often become close friends because of sharing a common life cycle. Baby clubs, family days, and other events provide an excellent opportunity to meet new people. At this point the couple's friendships often loosen with childless couples or individuals, even if they had been quite strong before, because of the completely different life situations.

- **Stronger social activity.** Many young parents feel the urge to engage in social or even in political life as a result of the birth of their child. They find their horizon stretched beyond their own lifetime, and they start to think about how to ensure a better future for their children. I have repeatedly observed parents becoming representatives in local government, or even opting for a higher political career, at this point in their lives.

How: Which Parenting Style to Follow?

John M. Gottman[3] started some exciting research in 1986. He examined 56 families with small children, spending 14 hours with each of them. They filled out questionnaires, participated in interviews, and took various medical tests. The study focused on the relationship between the parents, the handling of emotions, and the children's peer relationships. Later he involved more families in the study and observed them for more than two decades. The research divided the parents into four groups, based on their parenting style, and he observed that certain styles produced certain kinds of children over time. Let's examine the parental types.

- **Dismissing parents.** These treat the child's feelings as unimportant or trivial and want any negative emotions to disappear as quickly as possible. Because of that inclination, dismissing parents might ignore their children or even mock them. They show little interest in what the children are trying to communicate. Furthermore, dismissing parents may lack awareness of their own emotions, as well as those of others. Afraid of being out of control emotionally themselves, they are thus uneasy about the child's negative emotions. Regarding negative emotions as toxic, they perceive them as constant, unchanging traits of the child. It is hard to get dismissing parents to cooperate with the child in solving the problem that caused the emotion, as they expect that the passage of time will automatically solve it. Generally they downplay any triggering events for the child's negative emotions.

- **Disapproving parents.** The behavior of this type of parent can appear similar to that of the dismissing parent, but in a more negative way. Such parents judge and criticize the child's negative emotional expressions. They try too hard to set limits on emotional signals in the children and over-emphasize the rules, expectations, and standards of good behavior. Furthermore, they believe that bad feelings stem out of a bad character and assume that the child wants to manipulate them by using such negative emotions. Disapproving parents are convinced that the child has to obey under all circumstances and must submit to the parents' authority. Believing that emotions weaken a person, they try to raise the child to be tough in order to survive.

- **Laissez-faire parents.** Such parents exercise only a minimal influence on the child and let him or her develop as he or she wants. Laissez-faire parents freely accept all emotional expression from the child and offer comfort when they experience negative feelings, but they provide little guidance on behavior. Highly permissive (as opposed to restrictive), they don't have expectations about attitude or behavior and offer little or no instruction on how to solve problems. This type of parent is convinced that negative emotions cannot be handled other than through gratifying the felt need.

- **Emotional coach parents.** Here the parents value the child's negative emotions as an opportunity for intimacy and bonding. Able to tolerate spending time with a sad, angry, or fearful child, they are aware of and value such emotions. Emotional coach parents see the child's negative emotions as an exercise in parenting. Sensitive to their child's emotional states—even the subtle ones—they are not confused or anxious in the face of such emotional expression. Knowing what needs to be done, they respect the child's feelings and don't ridicule, and they do not tell the child how he or she should feel. Nor do they believe that they need to fix every problem for the child.

{parenting}

Although both of you may have a natural inclination toward a parenting style, you can freely and consciously decide which method you want to use in your family. Gottman's long-term studies have shown that emotionally intelligent parents raised the healthiest, most balanced children. Such children were significantly more successful at school, were ill less often, and cultivated better relationships with their peers than compared to children raised with the other styles. In addition, they had positive life expectations and better self-esteem. They were more able to work through a family crisis (e.g., divorce, loss), and when becoming adults, they were able to live in more stable marriages than the others.

Let's observe these four styles in a real-life situation. Imagine the following: While the family is doing the weekly shopping, their 6-year-old boy drops to the floor of the toy department and starts to scream that he wants to get the new toy all his other friends already have. The situation is extremely embarrassing—everybody around is watching. How will the various types of parents react?

The dismissing parent pulls the kid up from the floor with a red face and looks at him with a disdainful expression, as if he or she is embarrassed to be with him. In the meantime the parent tells him how badly he's acting and how intolerable and unacceptable that is. Unfortunately, that creates a distance between the parent and the child, as if the parent had nothing to do with how the child behaves.

The disapproving parent does the same as the dismissing parent, but when he or she raises his or her voice, it may appear to an observer that the adult is just as hysterical as the child. Then the parent threatens severe penalties if the child does not stop the tantrum, and it might also happen that he or she will administer some slaps right there in the shopping center.

The laissez-faire parent thinks that the solution is to give the child the toy. Therefore he or she does not direct his or her attention at the child's behavior, but at the possibility of purchasing the toy. To this parent the family budget, not the child's behavor, is the issue. The parent buys the toy right away or makes a promise that if the kid stops, he or she will get it on payday, etc.

The emotional coach parent takes seriously the wishes and feelings of the child, but does not feel compelled to buy the toy simply to eliminate the disturbing behavior. He or she picks up the boy from the floor, looks at him calmly, and speaks with a kind voice, saying something like "I see that this is very important for you. I also like new things, but we cannot buy everything the moment we see it. At home we will discuss the matter and decide what to do. Now we need to move on and look for the things on our shopping list."

If you want to explore your parenting style further, fill out the test in Gottmann's book *Raising an Emotionally Intelligent Child*.

What You Must Agree On

Before we move on I wish to highlight three areas couples rarely take into consideration before marriage, but ones that can later cause serious problems:

- **Parents or a couple?** It is better to determine beforehand—rather than after a child's arrival—to take care of your own relationship, cultivating each other's emotional well-being and sexual needs. Jürg Willi writes that "many parents tend to neglect their marriage and sexuality after the arrival of the child. They become a child-centered couple. As a couple therapist I experienced how important it is for the couple to find time and space in their marriage to nurture their relationship despite having children. It is fatal for the marriage if the couple is always together with the kids."[4] It is not selfish to leave the children with the grandparents and spend a weekend together. Some of the most important things that parents can give to their children are not necessarily even directed at them. Many parents love their children, but live in a tense relationship with their spouse, which causes the child to experience fear and uncertainty. The best thing that parents can do for their children is just to love each other! And that takes time.
- **Roles in child care.** This might seem trivial, but it can create many problems in real life. What is the role of a mother in child-rearing and what is that of the father? Since in most cultures the mother stays home with the children, it is important that the father also find tasks to contribute to child care (for example: evening bath, putting the child to bed, telling a bedtime story, etc.). It is also vital that the parents always support each other's authority in front of their children. Even if you do not agree, you should not discuss it in their presence. Always display unity when their eyes are on you! Children can masterfully take advantage if the parents' opinions differ. So set the rule in your family in advance *that you will never differ in front of the child.*
- **Discipline.** You both brought distinct customs of discipline from your own homes; therefore, it is a good idea to agree how to handle it before the child arrives. Concerning corporal punishment, Gottman observes:

"The problem is, a threat of spanking works too well in the short term: It stops misbehavior immediately, often without discussion, cutting off chances to teach the child self-control and problem solving. And in the long term, spanking may not work at all. . . . After a spanking, children are more likely to think about revenge than self-improvement. A sense of humiliation may cause them to deny wrongdoing, or they may plot ways to keep from getting caught the next time they misbehave. Spanking also teaches, by example, that aggression is an appropriate way to get what you want. Studies show that children who are hit are more likely to hit their playmates, especially those playmates that are smaller and weaker. . . . Research indicates that, in relation to the severity of physical punishment received, spanked children become more aggressive. As teenagers they are more likely to hit their parents.

"As adults, they are more likely to be violent and tolerate violence in their relationships. And finally, people who were physically punished as children are less likely to care for their aging parents."[5] Compared to spanking, a much more effective method is the so-called time-out.[6] The parent should respond with a quiet instruction to the unwanted behavior of the child. For example: "Daniel, collect your

{parenting}

cars *now*." The parent speaks calmly and in a normal voice in order for the child to learn that the parent is serious about what he or she says, even if he or she says it without raising the voice (though you may slightly emphasize the *now*). Many children will respond only when parents yell. If the child ignores the instructions, the parent should calmly say "One." Then the parent waits a few seconds in order to leave some time for the child to react. If nothing happens, then comes "Two." Do not start to count fractions ("one and a half," "one and three quarters"), because it takes away the seriousness of the matter. If still nothing happens: "Three! You're going to sit in the corner!" After counting to three, making the child sit in a corner is a very effective approach. Place the child on a chair in a remote corner of the room, where the parent can control him or her. In this case the penalty is not pain, as with spanking, but withdrawing attention. During the penalty no one initiates contact with the child—they will pretend that the child is not there. But withdrawing attention is not a license to make the child feel rejected. The child should sit in time-out for as many minutes as years of age. In the case of talking or hysterical outbursts, the time-out will start over. The initial use of time-out will demand a lot of patience on the part of parents as they seek to introduce the method, but after two or three weeks of "practice," it will feel as though the child has changed. This method is very effective because it does not simply punish the child for unwanted behavior, but also teaches him or her that the parent's word has weight, even without shouting.

• ***Spiritual education.*** Another issue requiring prior consultation between prospective parents is the child's spiritual and religious education. Spouses coming from denominationally mixed backgrounds should pay special attention to the topic. I hear the following from a growing number of practitioners and prospective parents: "We do not influence the child's belief. Let him decide for himself." In my opinion that is an impossible claim, which arises from the uncertainty of the parents. A child is never in a vacuum and doesn't grow up in a value-neutral environment, because he or she will encounter a set of values and a worldview even while in kindergarten! And consider the media, too. Whatever they experience in those areas they will consider as natural and valid. If the parents do not convey a worldview and a set of values or faith, then children will choose their own, based on whatever surrounds and influences them. In that sense there is no value-neutral parenting. The period before going to bed poses a great opportunity for faith education when spent in common prayer and Bible story telling or reading. It will become part of the child's evening bedtime ritual, and he or she will gladly remember it as an adult.

Exercise: How Much Do You Look Forward to Becoming Parents?[7]

Fill out the test, then compare and discuss the results.

Strengths are the items on which you both agree. On items 1, 2, and 5, circle those items if you both agreed (response 4 or 5). On items 3 and 4, circle the items if you both disagreed (response 1 or 2). Circle the strength items that you identify.

1. *Discuss your strengths and be proud of them.*

2. *Discuss the other items and decide how you can turn them into strengths.*

Response choices
1: Strongly Disagree
2: Disagree
3: Undecided
4: Agree
5: Strongly Agree

Statements	Bride	Groom
1. The father should actively participate in child-rearing and parenting.		
2. We have agreed on how we will discipline our children.		
3. Talking about parenting is stressful to our relationship.		
4. After we have children, we will give more attention to our children than to our marriage.		
5. We both look forward to becoming parents.		

Scoring (Score the quiz individually.)
(a) For items 1, 2, and 5, total your points: _____
(b) Add 12 _____ +12
(c) For items 3 and 4, total your points: _____
(d) Subtract (c) from (b) _____
Total points of the bride: _____ Total points of the groom: _____
Score range: 5-25

Interpreting your score:
21-25   You have many strengths in preparing for parenting.
15-20   Your preparation for parenting is generally good, but it could be improved.
11-14   Your preparation for parenting is good in some ways, but also needs improvement.
5-10   Your preparation for parenting needs improvement.

Get to Know Your Parenting Style

Fill out the parenting style test found in John M. Gottman's book *Raising an Emotionally Intelligent Child* (pp. 43-48). Although originally developed for mar-

{parenting}

ried couples, it will still give you insight and can facilitate conversation. Discuss the following questions.

1. *What will be the challenges of my style for me?*
2. *What will be the challenges of my style for my partner?*
3. *How can we support each other right now and develop an emotionally intelligent style?*

Methods of Discipline. The following exercise can help you discuss the issue of discipline, to exchange ideas, and to develop common principles and methods.

1. **What kind of methods did your parents use to discipline you?**

    The bride's experiences of disciplinary methods:

    _____
    _____

    The groom's experiences of disciplinary methods:

    _____
    _____

2. **Which one are you going to use as parents?**

    _____
    _____

3. **How will you support each other's authority in front of your children?**

    _____
    _____

---

[1] D. H. Olson, J. DeFrain, and A. K. Olson, *Building Relationships*, pp. 121, 122.
[2] Jürg Willi, *Was hält Paare zusammen?: Der Prozeß des Zusammenlebens in psycho-ökologischer Sicht*, 11th ed. (Hamburg: Rowohlt, 2008), pp. 88-90.
[3] John M. Gottman, *Raising an Emotionally Intelligent Child* (New York: Simon & Schuster, 1997).
[4] Willi, *Was hält Paare zusammen?*, p. 87.
[5] Gottman, *Raising an Emotionally Intelligent Child*, pp. 103, 104.
[6] Noel Swanson, *The Good Child Guide: Putting an End to Bad Behaviour* (London: Aurum Press, 2000).
[7] David H. Olson and Amy K. Olson, *Empowering Couples: Building on Your Strengths* (Minneapolis: Life Innovations, 2000), pp. 173, 174. Modified for premarital couples by Gábor Mihalec.

12

{ leisure activities: }
switching off the routine

Icebreaker Questions:
- What has been the happiest day of your relationship so far? What did you do on that day that made it an important memory?
- If money would not play a role, what would a really happy day look like? Talk about what you would do on this day from waking up until bedtime.
- What do you imagine to be a good evening out after you are married?

Despite economic pressures and all the responsibilities of life, you need time off to do some fun activities. According to one survey, an average European adult has four to five free hours a day.* Americans will have comparable leisure. What do you spend your free time doing, and how does it influence your relationship? How can you balance the leisure time spent together and separately? Let's discuss these questions in this short, easy section.

I and/or We?

A common misconception is that two people who love each other should spend every minute together, because extra leisure time spent apart is a sign of deterioration of the relationship. Let me illustrate this. Once I attended a three-day training program with some of my colleagues. After I got home, Dora asked me who was there. I told her that I had met Robert and Zoli, and shared a room with Laci. Then she started with the questions:

"Did Bob's daughter recover from her illness?" "Did Zoli's wife find a job?" "Did Laci get used to the new apartment?" I'm afraid my answers were quite monotonous: "I do not know."

Then Dora burst out, shocked: "Then what have you talked about for three days?"

At last she asked a question I could answer accurately: "I've learned about Bob's new computer, I can tell you exactly all the features of Zoli's mobile phone, and I can also list all the repairs on Laci's car in the past six months. Shall I go on?"

The lesson learned from the discussion was that no matter how much the two of us love each other, we will always have social needs that can be satisfied only by friends of the same sex. Men's favorite topics of discussion tend toward common interests, work, and gadgets (computer, mobile phone, cars). In contrast, women tend to prefer to discuss emotions, needs, family, and other relationships. We do not have to feel bad when our marital partner is not always able to meet our social needs—it does not mean that we do not love each other. The magic key is balance. Spend some leisure time together and some free time apart. It is good to have shared hobbies, but it does not matter if you have differences in leisure activities. The point is, do not let your hobby stand between the two of you and poison your relationship.

Sufficient Quantities of Quality Time

When spending time together, many think that it is not the quantity but the quality that counts. But that is only partially true. In reality it should sound more like: "Sufficient quantities of quality time." In my experience, a happy couple must have a special time together when they devote time exclusively to each other. It is difficult to say how much private time a couple needs, but as a point of reference I would suggest 30 minutes at the end of every day, an evening out every week, a full day away every month, preferably a weekend on a quarterly basis, and a holiday week in every year. If you want to spend time together, you have to make it happen! Otherwise, there will always be an urgent job or a problem in child-rearing that can threaten your private time. Enriching your relationship will, however, have a positive impact on your whole lives and will also enrich your work and child-rearing as well.

How Can My Spouse Be My Best Friend?

We love to spend free time in the company of friends, and who else could be our best friend than our spouse? Such a statement doesn't contradict the previous one, namely, that we still need friends of the same sex. I will conclude this chapter with two important factors that can be helpful for spouses to become best friends.

1. Make shared memories. Every lasting friendship is built on shared adventures that feed the relationship for years, if not for decades. Think of your friends and how you became close. You will remember persons with whom you have gone through a decisive experience, or share many memories in common. For example, there are the former classmates who used to sit beside us for eight years, a teammate from an old sports group, or a cousin who spent a few weeks every summer at your place. Even if you were not able to keep up an intensive relationship with them, you will still consider each other solid and faithful friends because you have gone through a wide variety of life situations together, and you can be sure of each other's goodwill, loyalty, and honesty. Marriage requires the same. It is not enough to perform the daily routine in the same place, or to simply solve the emerging problems together. We need to remember special events--to keep in mind the happy memories that bathed our otherwise everyday relationship in a glorious light. Therefore a trip is not wasted money. That is why a weekend away from normal life can do wonders. Even a night at a concert can become an intimate link.

2. Treat each other with special respect. I have observed how very tense couples often talk in a rude, cruel tone. The relationship of Frank and Janet is a typical example. When they fight, they lose control and start speaking in an insulting tone to each other. Actually, the tone is more hurtful than the words. But if in the heat of the debate Frank's phone rings and he can see from the caller ID that it is one of his colleagues, he starts the conversation with that person with a pleasant voice and beautiful smile, despite the yelling of the preceding moment. He politely listens to the colleague, apologizes if something bad happened, and kindly thanks his friend for taking his last shift. After all this he puts the phone down, and Dr. Jekyll turns back into Mr. Hyde. The color of his face starts to change, his eyebrows raise and cross, and he resumes screaming at his wife just as loudly as before. For those pairs who are friends of each other, it works exactly the opposite. It doesn't matter to whom they are speaking—when their phone goes off and their spouse is calling, one can hear a special tenderness in their voices. They reserve their kindest words and most beautiful gestures for their partner. Such kindness is not just reflected in their conversations, but permeates their whole attitude toward each other. And they know exactly what makes the other one sad and what causes him or her joy. They know their mate's best and

{leisure activities}

worst experiences, and their favorite and least-liked food. As they pay attention to each other they treat the other with special love and respect.

Exercises: Fun Time Menu

1. List characteristics that make an occasion . . .

   Fun:
   _____

   Romantic:
   _____

   Exciting:
   _____

2. List five leisure activities you would like to do:

   _____
   _____
   _____
   _____
   _____

3. Share your list with each other, one idea at a time, as you take turns.

4. Choose from each other's list an item you will do next week.

   The woman's choice from the man's list:
   What?_____
   When? _____
   Where?_____
   Preparations? _____

   The man's choice from the woman's list:
   What?_____
   When? _____
   Where?_____
   Preparations? _____

Planning a Day Out

Think about the following question: What would you do if you had a free day together without needing to worry about work or other responsibilities?

How would you spend it? What programs would you organize for yourselves? What would you like to eat on a day like that? Where would you go? Plan the day from morning until bedtime:

_____
_____
_____
_____
_____
_____
_____

Carry out this plan at the first opportunity!

*Monostori Judit, "Munka, szabadidő, időallokáció" (Tárki európai társadalmi jelentés, 2009), www.tarki.hu/hu/research/gazdkult/gazdkult_monostori.pdf.

13

relations:
taming your in-laws

Icebreaker Questions:

Think about each other's family members and relatives, then answer the following questions:

- What do I know about these people (in addition to their names)?
- Who of them is sympathetic to me, and who is less so? Why?
- How might such people have influenced my partner's life? Do they have any kind of influence on our relationship today?

Whoever gets married marries into a whole family. An old saying declares: "Observe the mother, marry the daughter!" Nowadays I observe too many couples that are concerned only with each other because of the ecstasy of love, and they no longer pay attention to parents, siblings, or grandparents. The truth is, whether we want it or not, these kind—and sometimes not so kind—persons are going to have an impact on our marriages.

"And He Leaves His Father and Mother . . ."

As old biblical wisdom says: "Therefore a man shall leave his father and mother and be joined to his wife, and they shall become one flesh" (Gen. 2:24, NKJV). Pronounced during the first wedding ceremony in the history of humanity, it was meant to serve to protect all marriages of all ages. The married couple ought to detach themselves from their parents and relate with an exclusive affection to each other for the rest of their life, forming a separate unit, "one body." In other words, the attachment that connects an adult man and woman in a marriage is more powerful than the connection they have as adult children to their parents! If you follow this principle, your marriage will be from a lot of unnecessary conflicts. In the Christian religious context the parents sometimes oppose this with the fifth of the Ten Commandments: "Honor thy father and thy mother!" And they believe that respect for the parents means that the adult (and married) child should allow them a say in everything in his or her life. But that is not true. The adult children have *responsibilities* to their parents, but they are not *accountable* to them. Salvador Minuchin explains the same concept in the language of a therapist: If two partners join with the intention of forming a family, this is the formal beginning of a new family unit. But many steps separate the formal initiation of a family and the creation of a viable unit. One of the tasks a new couple faces is negotiating their relationship with each spouse's family of origin. In addition, each family of origin must adjust to the separation or partial separation of one of its members, the inclusion of a new member, and the assimilation of the spouse subsystem within the family system's functioning. If the long-established structures of the families of origin do not change, they may threaten the processes of forming the new unit.[1]

Indirect Conflicts

A conflict with the family members of your partner can start in a number of ways. The most common one is what we could call an indirect conflict. We could classify such cases into a group of when the family member is not present himself or herself, but his or her "ghost" appears in the form of ideas, gestures, and intonation. They are the "You sound just like your father/mother!" situations. We must accept that we are influenced by our family of origin, and we can recognize bits and pieces from its traditions. The father-daughter and mother-son relationship reveal a lot about how you will function as a couple. My colleagues and I often observe, for example, that a woman who received little attention from her father and little positive confirmation as a young girl will find it difficult to relate intimately to her husband in adulthood. And a man who ended up in a role of emotional replacement because his mother's marriage grew cold will also have hardships in emotionally attaching to his wife. Even

{relations} 115

two- or three-generation-old "ghosts" can linger in a family. It can be a great tool to map these phenomena if you draw and discuss your families' genogram (family tree) as part of your marriage preparation. Such a diagram can answer many of your questions, and it helps you realize threats that may one day form stumbling blocks in your relationship (and can be turned into stepping-stones with a little care and hard work).

We suggest that when preparing the genogram you start with your relationship (a female is represented by a circle, a male is usually marked with a square); then both of you can move upward and add siblings, parents, grandparents, and so on. For the sake of clarity you can write names above the signs and numbers into the circles and squares according to the person's age. It is worth it to include deceased relatives as well, going back in time as far as you can to get a richer picture of your ancestors' relationships. You can mark those who have died with an "x" or by putting the date of death above their signs. In addition, you can show relationship dynamics through other signs. For example, you can indicate a divorce by a slash, and nonmarital relationships with a dotted line. The following fictive genogram displays a family with every possible sign.

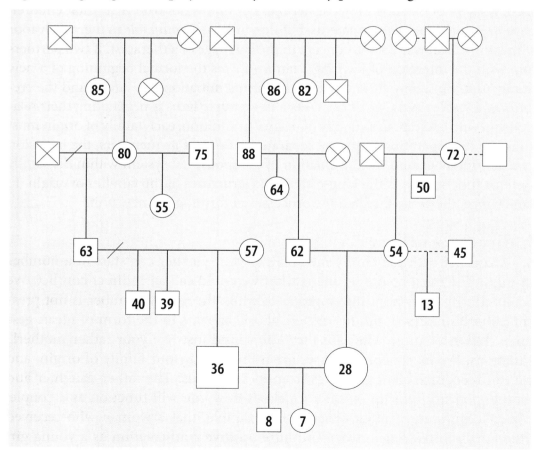

The above genogram portrays the family of a couple in which the husband is 36 and the wife is 28. They have two children, an 8-year-old boy and a 7-year-old girl.

The husband is the youngest of three brothers (his brothers are 39 and 40), the wife was an only child, but her mother had an extramarital relationship with a man nine years younger, from whom she has a 13-year-old son. The husband's parents are divorced, just as the husband's father's parents. Observing the wife's ancestors, we note a long tradition of extramarital relationships in the family, as her mother's mother, and also the father of her grandmother, established illicit relationships. The sample genogram is quite extreme, but it makes clear that in a marriage, both parties might carry dangerous patterns that will endanger even the relationship itself when they might find themselves in a deep conflict situation. The husband of the demo couple carries the idea that the easiest solution of marriage problems is a divorce, and his wife might have a hidden urge to look for a younger man to find comfort.

If necessary, you can get professional help to process your genogram and find the factors that may challenge your relationship. An experienced counselor can then help you develop appropriate management strategies for the odds you may be facing. The PREPARE inventory (www.prepareenrich.com) and the Couple Checkup (www.couplecheckup.com) online inventory specifically address the different joys and fears of each other's family, and you can benefit from what the tools reveal about the aspects of your relationship.

Direct Conflicts

These are the real-life situations in which the values, family traditions, tastes, or even interests clash with those of the spouse's family in the presence or absence of the partner. The most usual conflicts range between the wives and their mothers-in-law. That is because the two women are fighting each other for the love of a man, and the man stands in between and doesn't know whom to be loyal to. Gottman has a clear position on this issue:

"The only way out of this dilemma is for the husband to side with his wife against his mother. Although this may sound harsh, remember that one of the basic tasks of a marriage is to establish a sense of 'we'-ness between husband and wife. So the husband must let his mother know that his wife does indeed come first. His house is his and his wife's house, not his mother's. He is a husband first, then a son. This is not a pleasant position to take. His mother's feelings may be hurt. But eventually she will probably adjust to the reality that her son's family unit, where he is the husband, takes precedence to him over all others. It is absolutely critical for the marriage that the husband is firm about this, even if he feels unfairly put upon and even if his mother cannot accept the new reality. This is not to suggest that a man do anything that he feels demeans and dishonors his parents or goes against his basic values. He should not compromise who he is. But he has to stand with his wife and not in the middle. He and his wife need to establish their own family rituals, values, and lifestyle, and insist that his mother (and father) respect them. . . . An important part of putting your spouse first and building this sense of solidarity is not to tolerate any contempt toward your spouse from your parents."[2]

David and Vera Mace suggest the same:

"There is a golden rule that all married couples should try earnestly to follow in their relationship to their families of origin. It is: *Try never to allow your family members, or any one of them, to make critical judgments of your marriage, or of your marriage partner, when your partner is not present to hear what is said.* . . . When this happens, it nearly always causes trouble. Make it clear that you are open to receive helpful suggestions about how to improve your marriage relationship, because that will always be welcome. But you and your partner want to hear such suggestions together so that you can, if necessary, act on them together. . . . If suggestions about your behavior are, in fact, made by family members on either side to both of you together, always try to treat them seriously. If they seem not to be relevant, nevertheless take the trouble to explain carefully, and positively, why they are not acceptable."[3]

Although such conversations can be uncomfortable, sit down and talk to both of your parents about your future relationship, possibly even before the wedding! Discuss expectations and possible worries openly. Your parents may have expectations toward you that they will not tell you directly, but will feel offended when such expectations are not fulfilled (for example, that you must spend every Christmas with them). It is important to establish how you define your marriage compared to them, and what role you want them to play in your married life.

Work Toward a Positive Relationship

Despite all difficulties and conflicts, your families of origin can be a significant resource in your marriage, so it is worth paying attention and building a positive relationship with them from the beginning. Your parents love you, and they want you to live well (although they sometimes communicate that in strange ways). A good relationship with them can help your marriage in difficult times, and will be a great asset to your future child as well (as you might have good memories of your grandparents from your own childhood).

Exercises

Photo album and box. Talk to each other about experiences with your parents in childhood. List your memories, then select five that you will put into an imaginary photo album. Pick five other memories that you do not want to remember, and slip them into an imaginary box that will be put into the imaginary attic.

The bride's memories

Photo album

1. _____

2. _____

3. _____

4. _____

5. _____

Box:

1. _____

2. _____

3. _____

4. _____

5. _____

The groom's memories

Photo album

1. _____

2. _____

3. _____

4. _____

5. _____

Box:

1. _____

2. _____

3. _____

4. _____

5. _____

Farewell to the Status of a Child

I use this exercise as a compulsory one for couples preparing for marriage. The task will free a lot of emotion in parents and in the children preparing for marriage, but at the same time it initiates a whole new relationship between the parties. It can provide a good basis for balanced relations in the future.

Write a farewell note to your parents and find an intimate and quiet time before the wedding when you can read your letter to your parents (each of you to your own parents).

The following list may help you formulate your thoughts:
- I am grateful to you . . .
- What I have learned from you . . .
- Your marriage was a model for me in . . . (if it really was)
- What made me feel bad . . .
- I regret and would really want to mend . . .
- What I want from you in the future . . .

Making an Inventory of Each Other's Family

Think of your relationship with various members of your partner's family. If you feel that your spouse is not necessarily on your side in any of those relationships, or that ongoing issues exist with a particular family member, check the appropriate box.

The bride's inventory:
- ❑ my partner's mother
- ❑ my partner's father
- ❑ my partner's brother(s):_____
- ❑ my partner's sister(s): _____
- ❑ other family members:_____

My successes: _____

_____

_____

Remaining conflicts: _____

_____

_____

The groom's inventory:
- ❏ my partner's mother
- ❏ my partner's father
- ❏ my partner's brother(s):_____
- ❏ my partner's sister(s): _____
- ❏ other family members:_____

My successes: _____

_____

_____

Remaining conflicts: _____

_____

_____

---

[1] Salvador Minuchin, *Families and Family Therapy* (London: Tavistock Publications, 1977), pp. 26, 27.
[2] J. M. Gottman and N. Silver, *The Seven Principles for Making Marriage Work,* pp. 190-192.
[3] David and Vera Mace, *When the Honeymoon's Over* (Nashville: Abingdon Press, 1988), pp. 84-88.

14

{ roles and relationships: }
housekeeping in style

Icebreaker Questions:

- Who was dominant in your parents' marriage? Is there something you would want to learn from your parents' marriage concerning the sharing of leadership? What would you do differently?
- What do you think the role of a man and of a woman look like in an ideal marriage?
- How should a married couple share household responsibilities if both parties are working full-time?

When you have successfully sorted out mothers-in-law, then you have to come to terms with each other! The roles you play in your marriage will significantly contribute to the success of your relationship. As Olson puts it: "Happy couples are much more likely to not feel concerned that one partner is doing more than his or her share of household tasks than unhappy couples are. . . . Happy couples are much more likely than unhappy couples to agree that both partners work at having an equal relationship. Happy couples also tend to make decisions jointly and to allocate household chores based on interests and skills rather than traditional roles."[1] Two contradictory thinking modes clash on the subject: The traditional division of roles that men earn, smoke a pipe, and drink beer, and wives do the washing, cooking, cleaning, child-raising . . . and the egalitarian family model, in which both parties contribute their share of household chores, they both can build a career, they make decisions together, and they raise the children jointly.

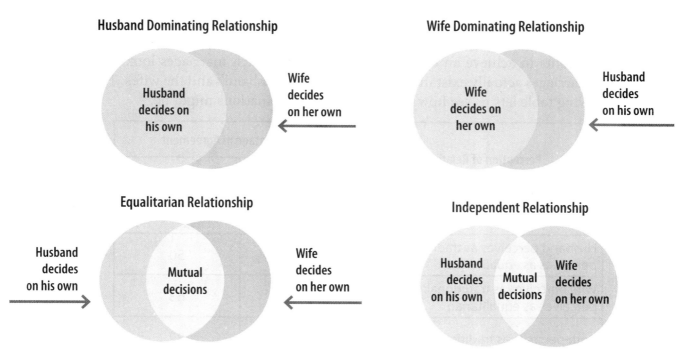

Who Has the Power?

The question significantly affects the interpretation of roles. The distribution of power within a marriage can occur as in the following four scenarios:[2]

- A husband dominates the marriage, in which the man is the boss and makes the decisions concerning the relationship.
- A wife dominates the relationship, in which the woman is the boss and makes the major decisions.
- An independent relationship, in which the parties are equal, but have little contact with each other. They make most of the decisions separately, and they engage in a parallel life alongside each other.
- An equalitarian relationship, in which the parties are close to each other and share equally in power. They make those decisions that affect their relationship jointly, while in other issues they accept that the other one has a right to make separate choices.

{roles and relationships}

Research has shown that the members of an equalitarian relationship are the most satisfied with their marriages. They are the most honest with each other, they will become the least depressed, and they have the highest degree of intimacy. In contrast, in couples with unequal relationship roles the more powerful partner is least satisfied with the relationship, is less honest, and feels that they lack intimacy in the relationship. The suppressed partner has problems with self-worth, is prone to depression, feels that the other is hostile, and is dependent on him or her.

Two Marriages: The Husband's and the Wife's

Since marriage unites the different lives of two people, it is not self-evident that both of them think similarly about their roles in marriage. Some couples do have similar perceptions, but in others one party is conservative while the other wants to achieve an equalitarian relationship. Such marriages look as if two marriages actually exist in the relationship: the husband's and the wife's. The following table lets us see how successful such combinations might be.[3]

Perception of Relationship	Percentage in Agreement	
	Happy Couples	Unhappy Couples
Both perceive as equalitarian	81	19
Husband perceives as traditional; wife perceives as equalitarian	50	50
Wife perceives as traditional; husband perceives as equalitarian	37	63
Both perceive as traditional	18	82

Subordination as a Religious Requirement?

A 28-year-old wife told me in a counseling session, "I am always tense. I also saw a psychiatrist. I'm taking medications because I simply cannot meet the requirement I have set for myself. My husband does not even expect this from me, but I know from the Bible that I must obey him in everything." Although space does not allow for a longer discussion of this issue, I would like to at least briefly address the question, one so often misunderstood by many Protestant and Evangelical Christians—who otherwise have fought for centuries for equality and freedom of conscience. I asked the woman where she read this requirement in the Bible, and she turned to Paul's letter to the Ephesians: "Wives, submit to your own husbands, as to the Lord. For the husband is head of the wife, as Christ is head of the church" (Eph. 5:22, 23, NKJV).

If we read only that sentence, it does seem that women have a subordinate role. But it is a typical example of snatching a sentence out of its context and interpreting it in a very different way than what the author originally intended.

I asked her to read the previous sentence. It reads as follows:

". . . submitting to one another in the fear of God" (verse 21, NKJV).

That puts the matter in a completely different light. In marriage, the parties should mutually obey each other, and this is the solid starting point after which the author details the roles he assigns to women and men. We already got to know the woman's part, so let's have a look at the man's:

"Husbands, love your wives, even as Christ also loved the church and gave himself for it" (verse 25). From this description we can draw the picture of a caring, protective, proactive man, and not the image of a dominant, bossy, and aggressive male.

Although in biblical times the superiority of a man was a socially accepted matter—which has an imprint also in the Bible—I feel free to say that *the Bible describes marriage as the full union of two equal persons, a man and a woman, who are different in their functions but equal in state and dignity.*

Let's Summarize It!

In conclusion, here are the differences between the two role models in more detail.[4]

Traditional	Equalitarian
one-vote system	two-vote system
fixed roles—differentiated by gender	fluid roles—based on personal choice and competence
husband provider—wife homemaker	flexible division of provider and homemaker functions
husband initiates sex—wife complies	sex initiated by either husband or wife
issues settled with reference to legalistic principles and rules	issues settled with reference to personal and interpersonal needs
wife close to children—husband disciplinarian and authority figure	husband and wife both close to children; both represent authority
husband assumes role of religious head of family	religious functions of family shared by husband and wife
further education important for husband, not for wife	further education equally important for both
husband's vocation decides family residence	family residence takes account of both husband's and wife's vocation

{roles and relationships}

Exercises

Household chores list. List as many household chores as you can think of and agree how you will share them (gardening, cooking, cleaning, child care, and organizing and scheduling). First, prepare a list separately and indicate whom you think should do the job. Compare the lists and agree on a final delegation that is acceptable for both of you. Record the results below:

Chores of the wife	Chores of the husband
1.	1.
2.	2.
3.	3.
4.	4.
5.	5.
6.	6.
7.	7.
8.	8.
9.	9.
10.	10.

Individual Ranking of Roles and Responsibilities

1. Fill in the empty lines with roles that need to be performed at this stage of your life (e.g., spouse, parent, sibling, child, employee, manager, club member, etc.).

2. Rank these roles according to their priority in your lives. To do this, use the squares at the beginning of the rows and write in numbers ranging from 1 to 10 that indicate your personal priority (1 = most important, 10 = least important). In case 10 lines are not enough, use a separate sheet to continue to list the roles as you see fit.

The bride's list of roles:

❑ _____
❑ _____
❑ _____
❑ _____
❑ _____
❑ _____
❑ _____
❑ _____
❑ _____
❑ _____

The groom's list of roles:

❑ _____
❑ _____
❑ _____
❑ _____
❑ _____
❑ _____
❑ _____
❑ _____
❑ _____
❑ _____

3. Look at each other's order of importance. I hope that both of you put the role of spouse among the first three places. If there is a conflict in the priorities between the two lists, now is a great opportunity to discuss the issue. Talk about how your partner's value system makes you feel, and reflect on what both sides could adjust in order to bring the positions closer.

[1] D. H. Olson and A. K. Olson, *Empowering Couples,* p. 79.
[2] D. H. Olson, A. Olson-Sigg, and P. J. Larson, *The Couple Checkup,* pp. 130, 131.
[3] Olson and Olson, p. 72.
[4] David R. Mace, *Close Companions: The Marriage Enrichment Handbook* (New York: Continuum, 1984), p. 16.

15

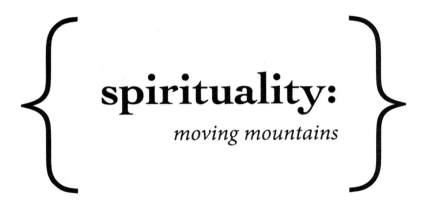

{ **spirituality:** *moving mountains* }

Icebreaker Questions:
- Did spirituality play a role in your family of origin? How did you celebrate religious holidays at home (Christmas, Easter, etc.)?
- How did you think about issues such as the meaning of life, what happens after we die, sin and forgiveness, or God?
- What are the spiritual values you would like to pass on to your children?
- If God were to enter your living room and wanted to give you something to particularly benefit your common journey, what would you ask for?

What have spirituality and faith to do with marriage preparation? In one survey 52 percent of European citizens could say: "I believe there is a God." Twenty-seven percent held that "there is some sort of spirit or life force," and only 18 percent answered, "I don't believe there is any sort of spirit, God, or life force." In the United States 70 percent of people claim membership in a church or synagogue, with nearly 90 percent of all adults indicating that religion is important in their lives.[1] Since it is an issue that affects so many, it needs to be addressed.[2] A person's faith orientation actually determines his or her value system, and values affect everyday behavior at all levels—including marriage. If that is so, the issue needs to be included in marriage preparation. In spite of this data, I excluded the term *religion* in the chapter's title, opting for the term *spirituality*. People commonly connect the word "religion" with formality and outward manifestation, but "spirituality" better reflects the subject of this chapter, since it is a more internal, intimate expression. All people have spiritual needs, but not everyone fulfills them the same way. Many people live out their spirituality in an organized ecclesiastical framework, but many others, who do not belong to any religious community, also try to meet their spiritual needs in some other form (esotericism, feng shui, meditation, etc.). In order to keep from excluding anyone from the topic, I will focus more on the content of spirituality than on a specific denominational teaching. However, since my own biblical Christian values have shaped my philosophy of marriage, I am influenced by this tradition.

The Effects of Spirituality on Marriage

Mr. and Mrs. Parrott write of marriage therapy:

"The spiritual dimension is a strong resource for the health and growth of a marriage relationship. No other factor is so significant in achieving unity and conviction in marriage than the spiritual values lived out together."[3] Although some may assume that they overemphasize their position, numerous scientific studies support it. For example, Larson and Olson examined 25,000 couples concerning their spiritual values.[4] They sorted the pairs into two groups based on whether they had high spiritual agreement (they showed harmony with each other's spiritual values and experience and/or had similar beliefs) or low spiritual agreement (they did not display harmony with each other's spiritual values, they were nonbelievers, or their beliefs were different from each other). The research revealed that couples who have faith and live out their spiritual values in a similar way scored higher in every relationship area than those who were nonbelievers or experienced tension in their spiritual values. The chart on page 130 displays the quantitative results.

Faith and spiritual values thus seriously affect a marriage, and they can be either an abundant resource for the relationship or a source of stress, depending on the spiritual compatibility of the partners. Another interesting result of the study was that the believing couples had less marital conflict, were more ready to cooperate, and were generally more satisfied with their marriage. In addition, the teenage children of believing parents showed less behavioral problems compared to those from a nonbelieving family. They also had better grades, were more willing to do volunteer work, and displayed more social responsibility.[5]

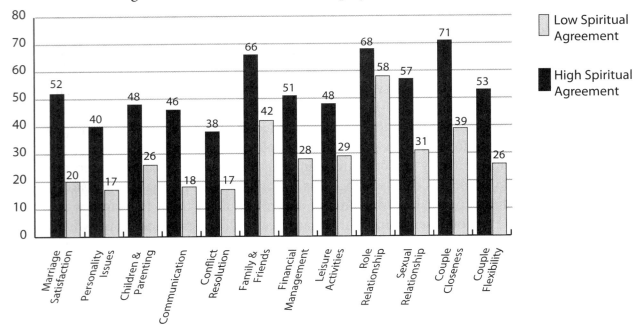

Compatibility

The word "compatibility" has become prominent in the world of computing. It means that two parts of equipment, made by separate vendors, are consistent with each other and can be linked. We can use the same term to refer to the spiritual values of a couple. Those who are compatible in their spirituality have a great advantage. Compatibility doesn't mean only that they both are believers, but that they both live out their spirituality in similar ways. If one is a devout Hindu and exercises a strict vegetarian lifestyle, and the other is a devout Catholic Christian and works as a butcher, they are likely to face a number of conflicts despite the fact that they are both devoted to their faith. That is the reason the Bible suggests that marriage should be a union between two persons of similar faith (and why many pastors or priests refuse to perform a wedding for denominationally mixed couples).[6] Interreligious marriages become especially problematic when at least one of the parties is active in his or her own denomination and practices his or her faith according to the teachings of that church. As Bochmann puts it:

"In my judgment, religious differences must be addressed when at least one party has strong roots in his or her own church. Faith and spirituality are much more than a matter of religious affiliation; however, religious affiliation defines them. For a believer, his own congregation and the church are always a bit of home, culture, and lifestyle—even if the person's behavior is critical of them. That is why this topic is more than 'just' doctrinal differences."[7]

We need to consider one more thing within compatibility issues that goes beyond religious affiliation: that men and women practice and experience spirituality fundamentally differently. Men are usually interested in external forms, which provide security in the intangible and immeasurable dimensions of spirituality. Thus teaching (dogma) and the order of formal worships are important for them. In contrast, women are more creative, more free, and more intuitive in the way they live out their faith. They often place greater emphasis on music, colors, and the internal content of worship.[8] Such differences are natural and do not mean that a couple is incompatible.

What Makes Believing Couples Even Stronger

• ***The concept of love.*** Couples who read the Bible seek to reach the highest standard of love. But what do we mean by love? The original Greek language of the New Testament Bible uses several words for love. Two of the most frequent ones are *phileo* and *agape*. The *phileo* is a friendly, more superficially focused love compared to *agape*, which is the initiating, committed, and self-sacrificing divine love. We see the differences between the two kinds illustrated by the following chart.[9]

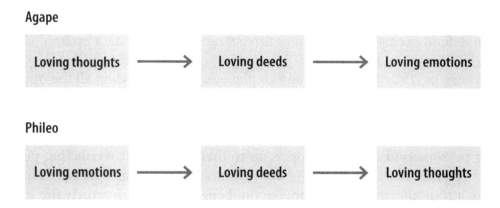

As you can see, the crucial contrast between the two kinds of love is that in *agape*, thoughts have primacy, while in *phileo*, emotions occupy the first place. Which one you choose to use in your marriage will have a direct impact on your relationship. The differences will show in conflict situations. When I quarrel with Dora, *phileo* dictates that emotions must hold first place. But in a conflict situation, the emotions (1) are not very positive. And if negative emotions will determine my acts (2), they will also be negative, so I raise my voice and might say unjust, even offending words. Finally, what I do will influence my thoughts (3), so I'm questioning if I still want to continue the marriage—all because of one conflict.

Let's change the script and begin with the thoughts (*agape*). If my thoughts (1) during disputes are at the beginning of events, it tells me that despite our disagreement, she is the one whom I choose to love and with whom I want to grow old together. It will define my actions (2), so what I'm going to aim toward is solving the conflict in a way that both of us will be winners: I will stay kind, I will not raise my voice, but I will try to understand her point of view and will

{spirituality}

show willingness to compromise. Then will come the emotions (3), which again will be passionate toward my wife. This is truly a process in which stumbling blocks can turn into stepping-stones, because we will end up closer to each other than before, and be even more committed to our marriage.

My counseling experience tells me that many divorces and acts of unfaithfulness occur because married couples base their decisions not on loving thoughts but on changing emotions.

• *God as a resource.* We all meet many challenges that will stretch us to the edge of our human capabilities. If you are facing them alone, you can get bitter and discouraged. However, if you've been a believer, you know that God works even beyond human possibilities, and that He is at your side to help you determine a solution when you may have already given up. A beautiful Bible verse (one often printed on wedding invitations) sums this up:

"Two are better than one, because they have a good return for their labor. If either of them falls down, one can help the other up. But pity anyone who falls and has no one to help them up. Also, if two lie down together, they will keep warm. But how can one keep warm alone? Though one may be overpowered, two can defend themselves. A cord of three strands is not quickly broken" (Eccl. 4:9-12, NIV).

A common effort can solve many challenges. However, when all the options run out, for the believer there still exists a mysterious third cord of the rope, which symbolizes God's invisible yet very real presence.

• *Prayer as a tool to deepen intimacy.* Several studies have shown that praying persons find it easier to open up to their spouses. It seems that prayer is a sort of practice in learning to share innermost feelings and thoughts in the presence of another person. In prayer the believer puts into words the kinds of things he or she would never say in front of others: shame, thanksgiving, wrath, doubts, confession, etc. The more the believer practices this in his or her relationship with God, the more natural it will feel to use this skill in human relationships (in marriage or parent-child situations). In addition, common prayer and Bible reading increase the couple's intimacy and commitment for each other. It is a beautiful symbol of becoming "we" when the couple can say together, "Our Father . . ."

Tokics Imre reflects on the language of theology: "When the New Testament calls humans 'anthropos' (a creature looking up), it doesn't do more than verbally highlight the fact that mankind has a religious inclination. We need to ask the question: What is the condition of becoming We for two independent individuals? The slogan of egoism is Me. A little more sophisticated version of this is when we get to pronounce: You and Me. However, true community starts with the word We. Our task is to arrive from Me to the higher-quality We state in different situations of life. In all initiatives where we are to achieve the real We community (God's), the Father's hidden presence will surface."[10]

Exercises

To believe or not to believe...

Since I do not know where you stand on the issue of faith, I have worded this exercise in two different ways. If you believe, meditate on what your faith contributes to your relationship. But if you do not believe, do a thought experiment and jot down how your relationship might change if you gave spirituality more importance in your lives.

The bride's thoughts:

___

The groom's thoughts:

___

What you would like to change in your spiritual life:

___

Values and Marriage[11]

Fill out the following exercise individually, then discuss the results together. Prioritize the following items on the list by assigning a number to every item based on the importance it plays in your life (1 = most important, 10 = least important).

The bride's priority list:
- ❑ God
- ❑ family
- ❑ church
- ❑ herself
- ❑ partner
- ❑ parents
- ❑ work

{spirituality}

- ❏ children
- ❏ leisure/hobby
- ❏ other: _____

The groom's priority list:
- ❏ God
- ❏ family
- ❏ church
- ❏ herself
- ❏ partner
- ❏ parents
- ❏ work
- ❏ children
- ❏ leisure/hobby
- ❏ other: _____

---

[1] Rosta Gergely, "Változó vallásosság Magyarországon." Forrás: http://forsense.hu/content/RostaGergely_ValtozovallasossagMagyarorszagon.pdf.

[2] D. H. Olson, A. Olson-Sigg, and P. J. Larson, *The Couple Checkup,* p. 147.

[3] Les and Leslie Parrott, *Saving Your Marriage Before It Starts* (Grand Rapids: Zondervan, 1995), p. 145.

[4] Peter Larson and David Olson, "Spiritual Beliefs and Marriage: A National Survey Based on ENRICH." Forrás: https://www.prepare-enrich.com/pe_main_site_content/pdf/research/beliefsandmarriage.pdf.

[5] Olson, Olson-Sigg, and Larson, p. 149.

[6] See 2 Cor. 6:14, 15, NKJV.

[7] A. Bochmann, *Praxisbuch Ehevorbereitung,* pp. 141, 142.

[8] *Ibid.,* p. 131.

[9] Christian A. Schwarz, *Der Liebe-Lern-Prozess* (Emmelsbüll: C&P, 1998), pp. 17ff. Adapted by Gábor Mihalec.

[10] Tokics Imre, *Az imádság himnusza,* 2nd ed. (Budapest: Advent Kiadó, 2010), pp. 30, 31.

[11] C. Morgenthaler, *Systemische Seelsorge,* p. 180.

16

{ boundaries: }
mind the gap!

Icebreaker Questions:
- Have you ever felt you were too close to each other and worried you might have sacrificed your individuality on the altar of relationship?
- What changes are you willing to make for each other and for the sake of your relationship?
- How did your parents express emotional attachment to each other? What would you like to use from their customs in your own relationship, and what might you avoid?

We have now arrived at the last "ingredient" in our study of a good marriage. While not actually a separate, full-fledged category but a relationship model, it affects all other categories. It acts as an invisible dimension.

We will explore family and relationship structures, or to quote a more scientific definition, "the invisible set of functional requirements . . . in the interaction of family members."[1] David H. Olson's research has helped make those invisible dimensions visible through his couple and family map. It displays the level of flexibility and closeness in the couple's relationship.

- *Closeness.* As was stated several times previously, the parties in a healthy relationship maintain a good balance between togetherness (we) and separateness (I). If the level of closeness is too low, there will be little loyalty, bonding, and intimacy in the relationship, and the members will live independent lives. Where the level of closeness is too high, the family members will be extremely codependent. It demands and expects complete loyalty, and there is too much we at the expense of I. The same idea is put in a more poetic form by Rainer Maria Rilke: "By accepting the fact that even between the closest human beings infinite distances still exist, a wonderful living side by side can grow if they succeed in loving the distance between them, which makes it possible for each to see the other whole against the sky."

- *Flexibility.* This dimension examines the balance between stability and change. Relationships with a low ability to alter or adjust will have rigid roles. The couple resists any change, and strict rules regulate their life. In contrast, couples with high flexibility will go into too many new directions. Their life is chaotic. The leadership lacks stability and reliability, and they may impulsively make hasty, often erratic decisions. The roles and the rules keep shifting dramatically.

Let's demonstrate the practical consequences of this state on a hypothetical couple, Jane and John.

The horizontal axis of the chart on page 137 displays closeness (ranges from disconnected to overly connected) and the vertical axis portrays flexibility (from inflexible to overly flexible). Both axes show five possible levels, and together they form 25 small squares. The lightest squares (in the center, a total of nine squares) indicate that the couple is balanced both in flexibility and in closeness. The darker squares (on the side of the chart, a total of 12 squares) indicate that the pair is somewhat out of balance in one of the indicators. The darkest squares (in the corners of the chart, a total of four squares) mark that the couple lacks balance in both closeness and flexibility. For extra clarity, the chart includes notes on the side and bottom, with numbers marking the different stages of the relationship cycle:

1. Intoxicated by love. Jane and John have been dating for nearly two years and are contemplating marriage. Their relationship to the axis of flexibility shows the value "very flexible," which is understandable, since they would do anything for each other. They would move for each other's sake, even to the other end of the country. On the axis of closeness we see "very connected," which is also reasonable, since they are in love and planning their wedding.

2. Newlyweds. Their relationship changes a few weeks after the wedding. First, instead of "very connected" the diagram displays the "overly connected"

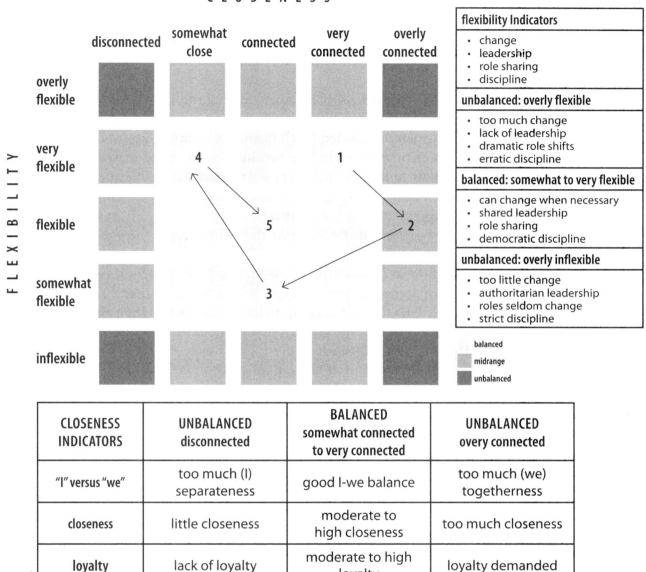

value. The couple's thoughts still revolve around the beautiful wedding day. They still feel the taste of the reception menu, and they would like to hold hands all day long. That is normal. But if they got stuck at this level, it would eventually pose a problem. We see a significant change in flexibility as well. Instead of the former "very flexible," the level dropped back one stage. The reason is that moving in together has resulted in a set of necessary rules that they had to adopt to maintain a peaceful coexistence (e.g., who does the laundry, who takes out the trash, who does the vacuuming, the ironing, etc.).

{boundaries}

3. The first years of marriage. Closeness settles into a balanced level after the early years (they can already imagine an evening without each other; John sometimes does things with his friends; and Jane has girls' nights out). Flexibility further decreases. Not only must the couple organize and regulate domestic duties, but they must pay the mortgage and make other important decisions.

4. The first child is born. A baby turns everything upside down (that's why I mentioned earlier that it is not fortunate when a baby comes early in a marriage). Every rule gets suspended (with flexibility jumping up two squares). They have to get up during the night, the furniture needs to be rearranged because of an increasingly mobile child, and new daily tasks arise. However, closeness is evaporating (John feels as if the little one has come between him and his wife—Jane is no longer a wife, only a mother).

5. The child is 4 years old. By the time the baby reaches the age of 4, the parents' marriage gets reorganized once more. They are able to concentrate not only on the child but also on each other, so they feel close again. Leaving the child with the grandparents for the weekend boosts their intimacy. Flexibility also regains a healthy balance, as the child no longer interrupts their nights, the house no longer looks as if a bomb had hit it, and the family returns to a more balanced, harmonious "normal" life.

What Can We Learn?

If we keep track of our family's life with the help of the couple and family map for a few years, it will prove that constant change is inherent in family life. This is normal, and healthy families can always reorganize themselves according to their actual life situation. Inflexible families will resist change. They do not adapt to life, but they want to bend life to their liking—and often fail. We must note, though, that the shifts of a healthy family will remain in the center of our chart, the lightest squares. It's true that for a moment it jumped into extreme closeness after the wedding, but if it's just a momentary overshoot and the couple don't get trapped in the extreme, it is acceptable and not dangerous for the relationship. Similar oscillations can occur because of sudden, traumatic events (accident, illness, losing a job). In such situations the family quickly reorganizes to deal with the problem more effectively. But then again, it will return to a healthy pattern. Scholars observed the phenomenon after the September 11, 2001, catastrophe in almost any American family's life.[2]

Research also sheds light on other interesting facts. Families that move around the center squares within the balanced area also have more positive communication than unbalanced families (think of the five-to-one ratio!). Such families can also work in the short term, in which flexibility or closeness (or both) follows an extreme pattern, but only as long as each member of the family accepts and supports the situation. If a family member steps out of the role and into an unbalanced state, it often results in the breakup of the family. Finally, balanced families have greater problem-solving skills, and they respond better to unexpected life events than unbalanced families do.

You may have already placed yourselves into one of the diagram's squares. Discuss where you see yourself, and how this affects your feelings. If you would like to use objective help, complete the exercises at the end of the chapter.

The Importance of the Family of Origin

If we go on (or actually back), we can place Jane's and John's families of origin on the couple and family map. We can draw several new lessons.

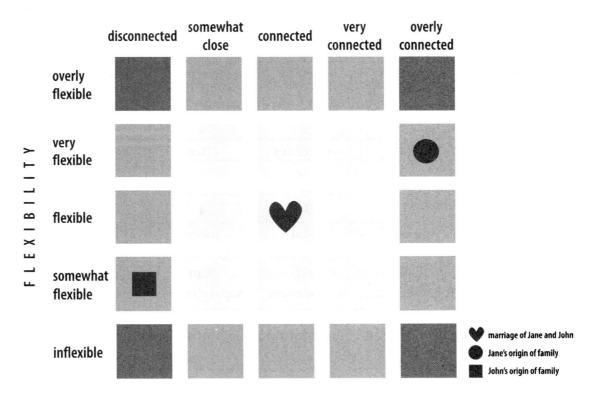

Let's continue where we left them in their life (stage 5). So much has changed, and we can see the family structure in which Jane grew up (very flexible, overly connected), and we also get to know John's family of origin (somewhat flexible, disconnected). Knowing the families of origin is important to a couple, as the partners automatically tend to follow the same pattern they inherited from home. For example, if John lost his job (a crisis that puts stress on the whole family), Jane will want to pull him closer (overly connected), but John would want to be alone (disconnected). If they do not know their couple and family map, this could be very scary for them, because aside from losing the job, they also perceive their marriage as in danger. However, knowing the patterns of the family of origin will aid them in understanding the dynamics taking place

{boundaries} 139

in their relationship, allowing them to rethink the situation and look for other solutions. The PREPARE or Couple Checkup inventories can provide accurate information on where your families of origin appear on the couple and family map. If you want to use them, fill out an inventory at www.couplecheckup.com.

Exercises[3]

Couple Closeness

1. How often do you spend free time together?

1	2	3	4	5
never	seldom	sometimes	often	very often

2. How committed are you to your partner?

1	2	3	4	5
slightly	somewhat	generally	very	extremely

3. How often do you feel close to your partner?

1	2	3	4	5
never	seldom	sometimes	often	very often

4. How do you and your partner balance separateness and togetherness?

1	2	3	4	5
mainly separateness	more separateness than togetherness	equal togetherness and separateness	more togetherness than separateness	mainly togetherness

5. How independent of, or dependent on, each other are you and your partner?

1	2	3	4	5
very independent	more independent than dependent	equally dependent and independent	more dependent than independent	very dependent

Add your responses to these questions to get a total closeness score.

Couple Flexibility

1. What kind of leadership exists in your couple relationship?

1	2	3	4	5
one person usually leads	leadership sometimes shared	leadership generally shared	leadership usually shared	leadership is unclear

2. How often do you and your partner do the same things (roles) around the house?

1	2	3	4	5
almost always	usually	often	sometimes	seldom

3. What are the rules (written or unwritten) like in your family?

1	2	3	4	5
rules very clear, very stable	rules clear, generally stable	rules clear, structured	rules clear, flexible	rules unclear, changing

4. How are decisions handled?

1	2	3	4	5
usually by one person	sometimes by both	often by both	usually by both	decisions rarely made

5. How much change occurs in your relationship?

1	2	3	4	5
very little change	little change	some change	considerable change	great deal of change

Add your responses to these questions to get a total flexibility score.

{boundaries}

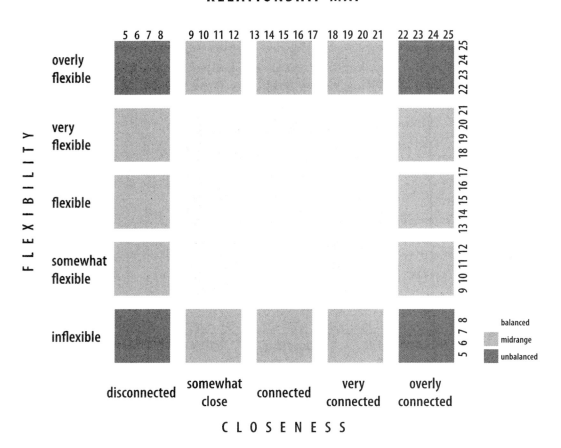

[1] S. Minuchin, *Families and Family Therapy*, p. 53.
[2] A. Bochmann, *Praxisbuch Ehevorbereitung*, p. 136.
[3] D. H. Olson and A. K. Olson, *Empowering Couples*, pp. 139-141.

17

{special issues in preparation for marriage}

Though we have already examined the possible dangers of a premarital relationship, here are some more specific situations that require the attention of therapists and must be addressed in the premarital counseling process.

Mixed Marriage of Denomination or Nationality

Religious communities judge the question of mixed marriages differently. Some do not regard it as an issue. Within the framework of premarital counseling, only the responsibilities of pastors of different denominations during the wedding ceremony need clarification. However, other communities seclude themselves from the possibility of members marrying someone of a different denomination, and they even anticipate the use of church discipline should someone do so.

Even though churches treat mixed marriages as a dogmatic question, from the point of the couple to be wedded it is primarily the issue of relationship dynamics, and only secondarily a theological one. "Unity of husband and wife in ideals and purposes is a requisite to a happy and successful home. The Scriptures counsel, 'Be ye not unequally yoked together with unbelievers' (2 Cor. 6:14). Differences regarding religion are likely to mar the happiness of a home where partners hold different beliefs, and lead to confusion, perplexity, and failure in the rearing of children. . . . Worship of God, Sabbathkeeping, recreation, association, use of financial resources, and training of children are responsible components of happy family relationships. . . . An adequate preparation for marriage should include premarital pastoral counseling in these areas."[1]

From the point of the couple's relationship, then, the living, the expressing, and the effect of their belief in their everyday life are primarily significant. They are questions that they need to deal with during wedding preparation. According to the earlier-mentioned research of Larson and Olson, the most important feature for a couple—concerning the issue of faith—is to agree in the practical expression of religious values and beliefs. In the representative examination involving 21,501 couples, 89 percent of the couples living in a happy marriage showed high correspondence in this category.[2] Olson's analysis also deals with the fact that only 5 percent of couples with low spiritual agreement (who live their beliefs differently) belong to the most satisfied relationship type (vital couples, four-star relationship), as opposed to the 36 percent of religiously compatible couples. He explains the success of the 5 percent as the result of the couples having learned how to manage their differences so well that they can apply it to their religious life.[3]

The same applies to differences in nationality. Bochmann (who lives in a mixed marriage of nationalities himself) observes that language and cultural differences in marriage can offer "richness if these are recognized and acknowledged as such, but become a great danger if they try to pretend that love covers all differences."[4]

He places special emphasis on the issues of language and culture in the case of mixed-nationality marriages. The issue of language is important because it can hinder communication between the members, which automatically weakens the relationship. Since it is harder for one to open up on an emotional level in another language, the difference may hamper the formation of intimacy. When speaking of cultural differences, couples especially need to explore the following aspects during the preparation discussion: "What role does the woman play in the given culture? How strong is the family cohesion? Is a small family, or a big family including more than two generations accepted? Who is the head of the family? What demands exist regarding visiting each other's acquaintances? What extent of closeness is accepted in the given culture? . . . Which is the dominant religion in the partner's culture? What religion does she/he follow? What political and ethical norms dominate in that culture? What is the characteristic way of clothing?"[5]

In the case of mixed nationality marriages when one partner is an immigrant, the couple must consider still another factor: the phenomenon of culture loss.

"Culture loss is a part of socialization, which involves both conscious and unconscious learning processes. During this, the person adopts the cultural traditions (e.g., language, value system, role models) of a society (or subsociety) and becomes a member of the new society."[6]

> The most important feature for a couple—concerning the issue of faith—is to agree on the practical expression of religious values and beliefs.

The immigrant gives up his or her own culture, and the effects of that will especially manifest themselves in the upbringing of children. Children born in mixed families will meet the culture of the immigrant parent's only in an indirect manner, thus behavior, thought processes, and value system will predominantly be shaped and defined by the context of the current culture.

Finally, in the case of mixed marriages formed through immigration we have to keep in mind that the immigrant member in some sense becomes dependent on the partner. Language knowledge, social bonding, and cultural embedding may be defective, and thus often the immigrant can connect to his or her new culture only through the spouse.

Ages of the Parties

In regard to age, three problematic situation groups can occur: (1) a couple younger than average, (2) a couple with a large age difference, and (3) a new couple of mature age. This subsection will look at the challenges of each situation.

According to research studies, a marriage age under 20 counts as a special risk factor,[7] and developmental psychology explains why: this age is the borderline between adolescence and young adulthood. The psychosocial crisis one struggles with in adolescence is the "identity or role confusion." If the young person successfully meets this crisis, he or she will be able to think about himself or herself as a unique person in a homogeneous picture. Next comes the psychosocial crisis of young adulthood known as "intimacy or isolation." After working through this, the young person will be ready and able to form close and abiding relationships.[8] But should the order reverse and the young person first choose a partner and then struggle with identity, it can create a wedge in the relationship. "Those adolescents who did not yet establish a fulfilling identity will have difficulties in participating in an intimate and mutually fulfilling relationship because their deepening in themselves makes it difficult to pay attention to the needs of the other."[9]

Turning to second group, the biggest challenge for couples with significant age difference is that the life cycles of the parties are out of sync. Because they are in different stages of developmental psychology and have different crises to solve, they live their relationship differently. Hans Jellouschek, a German couple therapist, states:

"Here is the point where the relevance of synchrony and diachrony in life cycles in regard to the relationship become apparent. The big age difference can cause a strangeness between the parties that is unbridgeable on the relationship level, and which is too easily ignored in the phase of being in love."[10]

The absence of harmony can make the relationship especially vulnerable for "outside interlopers." If the misstep of the younger spouse happens with a person of his or her age, it is especially hurtful and humiliating for the older spouse.

A number of years ago Hans-Joachim Thilo drew our attention to the risks of such choices.[11] According to Thilo, in the case of couples with significant age differences the younger party wants to experience something with the older partner that he or she missed receiving from his or her parents as a child. Such marriages may seem harmonious in the beginning, but after 10 to 12 years, serious conflicts may appear when the party who was damaged in childhood "grows up" and starts to act like an adult, while the party fulfilling parenting functions finds themselves stuck in the role and unable to handle the partner as an equal party. It is worth dealing with this issue during marriage preparation and is important for the couple to foresee future challenges within the relationship (decreased attractiveness, vitality, or sexual ability of the older party, etc.).

Mature-age couples have to face other issues during marriage preparation (aside from their relationship) that come from the current stage of their lives or health conditions and will influence their future marriage. These topics appear as separate categories in Olson's marriage preparation and marriage enrichment inventory pack that he developed for mature-age couples (MATE) as well. Such topics may group around the change-of-life stages (retirement, empty nest, etc.), transgenerational issues (the mature-aged couple is in a "sandwich" situation between adult-age children from a possible previous marriage and aged parents of their own who need to be taken care of), and health.[12]

Blended Family

Blended families (sometimes called "stepfamily" or "patchwork family") are those in which at least one of the parties has children from a previous relationship. They can become the typical "Your child and my child are beating up on our child!" situations. Such family combinations show distinct structural differences when compared to traditional family structures:

"(1) In stepfamilies, at least one of the important connecting persons for the children does not live in the family community. (2) Every member, or almost every member, has experienced the loss of an important connecting person (or a significant relationship form). (3) The stepparent (and in given situation, his or her children) has to find their place in a group living in existent, solid relationship patterns, and the two family parts need to grow together. (4) The children are part of more than one family community, they are members of the first and the stepfamily, but in given situations also have bonds to the family of the parent living in a different household who also established a new family. (5) One of the parents does not have parental rights toward one or more children and is a part of the parental subsystem."[13]

The members of the families in the process of formation need to deal with such differences consciously. The most frequent mistake is that the new family to be assumes that in this new situation everything needs to work like a "normal" family. The stepparent takes over the role of the biological parent, which often creates conflict. Instead, it is better if the stepparent does not try to be a supplementary parent, but puts on the role of a kind relative (uncle, aunt, etc.). On average, a blended family needs five years for achieving a balance.[14]

Cohabiting Couples Preparing for Marriage

According to the representative research of Pongrácz and Spéder, 67.9 percent of the citizens of my native country between ages 19 and 39 assume that the best way to prepare for a marriage is living together beforehand.[15] Unfortunately, the truth is exactly the opposite—it intensifies the risk of divorce. "Paradoxically, living together before marriage, which in some circles has almost become a norm under the assumption that the parties can then get to know each other the most thoroughly before marriage, actually increases the likeliness that such relationship will end with a divorce."[16]

Often I meet couples that already live together during marriage preparation. In such cases I need to give special attention to aspects that arise from the different dynamics of cohabitation and marriage. All of them result from the fact that the level of commitment is lower in cohabitation than in marriage, and those who lived together in such an arrangement carry this lesser commitment with them into the marriage. This issue especially surfaces at two points: (1) conflict management and (2) sexual fidelity.

Many studies reveal that the conflict resolution patterns a couple will most likely practice throughout their relationship will stabilize during the first two years of cohabitation.[17] In this respect it is vital that the couple—in terms of future conflict resolution—be committed to each other from the beginning of their living together. Billingham pursued a study closely related to this in which he showed that the lower the level of commitment, the more likely the parties will use verbal and physical violence in resolving conflicts.[18] It could be the reason that, in some subcultures, couples in a cohabitation relationship are three times more likely to experience physical violence than those living in marriage.[19]

We can note a curious attitude in connection to sexual fidelity in cohabitation relationships as well. In cohabitation the parties expect sexual fidelity from each other but at the same time demand a greater personal freedom for themselves than typically accepted in a marriage.[20] Since marriage changes the legal status of the parties but does not reform their way of thinking, marriage preparation needs to address such topics.

{special issues in preparation for marriage}

Summary

While systematically listing the risk factors influencing a marriage's success, I did not want to be discouraging. Instead, I wanted to urge caution. The success of a marriage depends on good preparation and being intentional about one's relationship. Both the couples and the professionals helping to prepare them for marriage can benefit from a detailed consideration of the many factors that affect marriage.

---

[1] *Seventh-day Adventist Church Manual* (Hagerstown, Md.: Review and Herald Publishing Association, 2005), pp. 182, 183.

[2] Peter J. Larson and David H. Olson, "Spiritual Beliefs and Marriage: A National Survey Based on ENRICH," www.prepare-enrich.com.

[3] *Ibid.*

[4] A. Bochmann, *Praxisbuch Ehevorbereitung*, p. 144.

[5] *Ibid.*, pp. 145, 146.

[6] Katharina Zoll, *Stabile Gemeinschaften: Transnationale Familien in der Weltgesellschaft* (Bielefeld: transcript Verlag, 2007), p. 207.

[7] Cf. D. H. Olson, J. DeFrain, and A. K. Olson, *Building Relationships*, p. 48.

[8] Rita L. Atkinson, Richard C. Atkinson, Edward E. Smith, Daryl J. Bem, Susan Nolen-Hoeksema, *Psychology*, 2nd ed. (Budapest: Osiris, 1999), pp. 99-101.

[9] *Ibid.*

[10] Hans Jellouschek, *Warum hast du mir das angetan? Untreue als Chance*, 10th ed. (München: Piper, 2010), p. 69.

[11] Hans-Joachim Thilo, *Ehe ohne Norm? Eine evangelische Eheethik in Theorie und Praxis* (Göttingen: Vandenhoeck & Ruprecht, 1978), pp. 168, 169.

[12] Cf.: David H. Olson, *Handbuch für Berater: PREPARE, PREPARE MK, ENRICH, MATE*, 3rd ed. (Neuenhagen: CAB-Service, 2006), p. 16.

[13] Manfred Cierpka, *Handbuch der Familiendiagnostik*, 3rd ed. (Heidelberg: Springer, 2008), p. 216.

[14] Doris Märtin, *Love Talk: Der neue Knigge für zwei* (Frankfurt am Main: Campus, 2007), p. 183.

[15] Pongrácz Tiborné, Spéder Zsolt, "Élettársi kapcsolat és házasság—Hasonlóságok és különbségek az ezredfordulón [cohabitation and marriage—similarities and differences]," *Szociológiai Szemle* 4 (2003): 55-75.

[16] Gödri Irén, "A házasságok és az élettársi kapcsolatok minőségének és stabilitásának néhány metszete [some segments of the quality and stability of marriages and cohabitation relationships]," in Pongrácz Tiborné, Spéder Zsolt (Szerk.), *Népesség—értékek—vélemények [Population—Values—Opinions]* (Budapest: KSH NKI Kutatási jelentések, 2002), p. 73.

[17] Cf. M. A. Fine and J. H. Harvey, *Handbook of Divorce and Relationship Dissolution*, p. 205.

[18] Robert E. Billingham, "Courtship Violence: The Patterns of Conflict Resolution Strategies Across Seven Levels of Emotional Commitment," *Family Relations* 36 (July 1987): 283-289.

[19] A. V. Horwitz and H. R. White, "The Relationship of Cohabitation and Mental Health: A Study of a Young Adult Cohort."

[20] Thomas Domanyi, "Eheähnliche Lebensgemeinschaften im Lichte der biblischen Ethik," *Dialog* 11 (2007): 2-5.

18

{ life stages of marriage }

As we can divide human life into smaller units or life stages (from infancy to old age), a marriage has its own span, a process that moves along through the years. All couples go through similar experiences so that the dynamics of the relationship show several common features. It is good to know those four life stages, along with their challenges, for several reasons:

• *We will not be overwhelmed by the small, everyday crises, but can place them into a bigger context.* For example, the way you argue and the subjects of those quarrels could be completely natural in the given stage and therefore you as a couple do not have some great, unfixable problem but are only moving through a particular life period.

- *It shows the possibility of continuous development.* The perfect marriage is not a constant state that starts on the day of the wedding and continues until the end of one partner's life. It is more like a growth process, one that matures through effort and conscious attention. If you plant a tomato seed today, it is unrealistic to expect to pick a fresh, juicy tomato for tomorrow's breakfast. However, if you know the natural trend of growth for the plant, you can develop patience and can wait for the fruit.
- *Knowing the course of growth makes one single-minded.* As we have determined several times, marriage does not only mean parenting, going to work, mowing the grass, and making love—it also (and mostly) means that two people realize a common life for themselves. When a couple creates their own culture, one in which they respect each other's goals and values, as well as the roles connecting them to each other, they establish a life community. And that it is much easier to achieve if not only the goal is in front of them, but also the map of the road ahead.
- *It will be easier to deal with transitions.* Because every life stage has its challenges and teachings, you have the opportunity to consciously speed up the course of one stage and then step into the next, because all stages point toward an ultimate goal: an orderly, balanced, war-free, rooted-down, and loving relationship.

Which stages will you be meeting through the course of marriage?
1. Dream Stage
2. Disillusionment Stage
3. Discovery Stage
4. Deepness Stage

The Dream Marriage

Ben and Susan were married yesterday. The ceremony was perfect, the mood was overwhelming, the honeymoon is glamorous, and everything is simply fantastic. And it is going to be like this from now on. No one is going to be able to challenge the love they have for each other, as the basic features of their relationship will always be passion, exclusiveness, and merging into each other. At least this is how they currently think. Parents and friends of the couple smile at them and their naïveté, because they have already gone through what the newlyweds are experiencing right now. *Just wait for it . . . it will change!* they think to themselves.

After the honeymoon normal life begins. Ben returns to his job, which takes up most of his time. Susan has already asked her boss before the wedding to employ her part-time so she would have more time for her husband, which she manages to achieve. Working until early afternoon, she then goes grocery shopping and straightens the house so that Ben can come home to a shining, nicely cleaned house. She makes dinner and serves it enthusiastically. The following conversation happens over the dinner table:*

Susan (*putting a plate on the table with toast and a fried egg cut in the shape of a heart, with green-pepper garnish cut into flowers*): I am so happy that you arrived home. I have made you a delicious toast and fried egg, just the way you love it.

Ben (*looks at the food and tries to avoid memories of his mother's stuffed cabbage*): Oh, honey, I love toast! And how attractively you serve it. None could make it more beautiful!

During dinner they both give a detailed account of their day's experiences, and professional eyes could see that they make many confirmatory gestures toward each other. Susan does everything she can to help her husband feel at home. She wants to provide warmth and belonging. Ben recognizes Susan's (seemingly quite modest) culinary knowledge, thanking her politely, and following dinner with a kiss and some endearing words. After dinner the conversation continues like this:

Ben: Honey, I have a great surprise for you tonight. I am going to take you out! I have booked a racquetball court at the rec center.

Susan: That will be great! (*Oh, no! I hate ball games! I was hoping we could work in the garden together.*)

Even though we have already gained insight on some specifics of the stage through the previous scene, let's arrange them into points:

• ***Glittering.*** Aptly named, in this stage everything is like a dream come true. The couple live in naive innocence, like Adam and Eve in Paradise. Their acquaintances are in one way sorry for them because of their rose-colored outlook. At other times, however, they are envious of them because the couple have achieved something in their naïveté that every person wants to have in his or her heart, and most of them have either never had the opportunity to experience it or have already lost it.

• ***Expectations come from experiences during courtship.*** While the rules of living together have not yet been fixed in their minds (though the dream stage can range from two to 10 years), they have achieved a tentative background as a result of their experiences during dating. But that can be a distorted reality. During dating we always see the other as attractive, relaxed, with fresh breath, and well groomed. Living together reveals that our loved one can have bad breath, snores sometimes, or does not clean up after himself or herself.

• ***Fear of negative feelings.*** Strange things can take place in the feelings between the couple. For example, spouses feel themselves responsible for each other's emotions, but they should not always do so. If the wife is sad, it is not necessarily because the husband could not fulfill her needs—so she does not need him to bustle around her but to sit next to her and just listen.

• ***Avoiding conflicts at all costs.*** It is also typical that the newly married flee conflict in a panic, because its presence might suggest that they are not as good a couple as they had envisioned. As a result, they start sweeping things under the rug until a huge bump in the middle of the room makes them trip.

• ***Putting personality aside for the sake of the dream.*** In the dream stage there is only "we," and the "I" gets put aside. Neither can imagine a night without each other, and they go everywhere together. They need time until a good balance forms between togetherness and being alone, when the husband can freely go to the gym with his friends and the wife can slip out for dessert with her friends without reproving glances from a jealous spouse.

• ***They do not love each other—instead they love the dream images of each other.*** A significant difference exists between who the other person is, that is, looking at him or her objectively (if it is possible), and the spouse's mental image of him or her. The two can even be the opposite of each other. In the dream stage they do not know each other so well that they could love each other for themselves, but they are in love with the mental picture they have painted of the other. All their common experiences soon strengthen or modify the picture, and they can then either begin to love each other more and more deeply and consciously, or they start to drift further away from each other and question the validity of their choice. In the stage of disillusionment they can arrive at a point where more "don't like" things exist in the other than "like" aspects, and temporarily the dream breaks. It is the job of the subsequent stages to form a new image of each other that is more realistic, and that they can love unconditionally. All in all, the dream stage is a beautiful part of a marriage. It is typified by such remarks as:

"I love you."

"I have to be beside you."

"I will not leave you ever."

"You are always going to be the first of everything to me."

"We love each other."

The Disillusioned Marriage

We have compared the first stage of a marriage to dreaming. Everything seems covered in pink clouds. By nature, though, dreams always end, and we wake up. But cheer up: if you have awakened from the dream, that is a sign of life! And we need at least this small sense of achievement in this stage. "How did we end up here?" is the main question of the couple, who suddenly find themselves in a previously unknown situation. What does a disillusioned couple normally look like? Maybe they are the ones you may know best from films. The marriage crisis is a frequent plot in movies. The couples are typically 30 to 40 years old and parents of one or two children. The husband spends a lot of time away from home, and the wife smiles remarkably little. Their time together is mostly limited to nighttime, somewhere between putting children to sleep and falling asleep while watching TV.

When does the dream end? There is no set time limit. Some couples find the "dream" ends after one to two years, but I have met a couple whose "dream" lasted 10 years. Signs of transition to the disillusioned stage are:

- *Arrival of children.* Kids do not come because the relationship has weakened, but if it is not stable enough, it can fade after the children arrive. It is natural that most of the attention focuses on the baby, and the spouses function more like a parent couple than a married couple.
- *The wife starts to fight for her rights.* The partners have so far handled everything that has surrounded their relationship with great flexibility. They were ready to make big sacrifices for each other and selflessly to subordinate themselves for the goals, job, and taste of the other. Now, however, suppression breaks to the surface and cries for equality. Because the woman commonly makes more sacrifices—often as a result of motherhood—it is usually she who first gets fed up with the situation.
- *Conflicts previously avoided now rise to the surface.* In the dream stage a couple may have compulsively avoided conflict. They refused to accept anything that might have suggested their relationship was imperfect. This process, of course, results in negative feelings swept under the rug. By now, however, the time has come to face the swallowed conflicts. In this situation the contrast between the previously imagined life without conflict and the present amount of argument can seem immense.
- *The husband does not invest the same amount of time and attention in the marriage and family.* Avoidance behavior is characteristic of this stage, something most commonly noticed in the husband. Not because he is worse, but because it is easier for him to slip into the habit because of his position. Since he spends the biggest part of the day outside the home, he can easily expand his working hours by indulging in friendly conversation with his associates. Then at home he can try to prepare a habitat in which he can avoid thunderstorms—places usually found near a television, computer, or other electronic device.
- *Persuasion, blaming, evasion, nagging.* Living parallel lives leads to the couple drifting apart emotionally. As a result, during a heated argument they can start employing expressions previously unimaginable to them. A marriage is like an old peasant's house surrounded by two courtyards. The one in the front looks fancy from the outside. The couple speak much "my love" and "honey" there. And at the back, the farm courtyard, which is not so orderly, there lives the "chick," the "swine," and the "cow." Ben and Susan have recently celebrated their fifth anniversary. Or they would have celebrated it, but before they left for the restaurant, Ben, on vacation from work, rocked his 2-year-old son in the swing in a way that the boy hit his head, which threw everyone into a panic, and they spent the lunch break at the doctor's. While they were waiting for the physician, Susan had a great opportunity to tell her partner how irresponsible a person he was, someone who does not even know how to deal with the child because he does not even know his own son—he is always working. Ben was about to answer her outburst, but they were suddenly called into the doctor's office.

A typical night in their lives goes like this:

Ben (*arriving home from work and in a not-too-friendly voice shouting*): "I'm home!"

Susan: I've made toast and scrambled eggs. I've had a difficult day. The child is ill—he vomited on me two times today. The toaster we got for a wedding present is starting to give up. It smokes like a chimney. Be careful with the eggs. I had to hurry, so a bit of an eggshell might have fallen in them.

Ben (*to himself*): *Oh, no! I can't even look at eggs and toast. When is she going to learn how to cook? I don't want to eat eggs and toast until I die! Even my secretary cooks better than she does.*

The child starts to cry twice while Susan tries to iron some of the clothes. Ben eats the scrambled eggs with a bored face and thinks about what might be on ESPN that night.

After the meal the two of them continue the conversation.

Ben: Honey, tomorrow night I'll be home late. The guys and I have rented a racquetball court and will play a few games.

Susan: But you promised me that we would go to the gardening shop to choose a new variety of rose!

Ben: Oh, the rose will be there the day after tomorrow, won't it? You know, I wouldn't mind if a jungle would grow in our garden. I don't even understand why you have to spend so much time and money on such things!

Susan: And why do you spend that much time and money on your stupid little rubber balls that you hit against the wall?

This couple really has to be careful of what they let themselves do in an argument. What they say in anger today will probably be the starting point for the next day. And if they want to give a greater emphasis to their words the next day, they resort to each other's "mothers," and not much time will lapse before the first slap. Most of the time couples divorce at this stage. However, the dream stage will end sooner and sooner in every successive marriage, and the parties will reach disillusionment as well. So instead of divorce, they should pay attention to what this stage wants to teach them. They must learn to love the person's true identity and not to feed the picture they have painted of each other in their minds. Thinking through the specifics of the stage, we could define the common phrases of the disillusioned marriage like this:

"I still like you, but . . ."
"But something must change!"
"I need space . . ."
"I need respect . . ."
"I need not just to be 'us' but to be 'me' as well.
"We are fighting with each other."

The Discovering Marriage

After the dream and disillusionment phases, discovery will finally start in the life of the couple. How sad it is that almost half of married couples never reach this stage in their life. Most slip into despair and give up during disillusionment. But if they could recognize that it is a totally normal thing that they are going through; if someone could just tell them that however futureless their situation looks at the moment, a time will come when they can believe in each other and feel an irresistible desire to grow old together; and if someone could show them a picture of a more harmonious future, the disillusioned couple would surely grab each other's hands more tightly and start to work on their relationship more consciously than ever. Should they manage to do so, they would rediscover their partner and begin a stage with similar dynamics to what they experienced in the dream phase. But because it does not suffer from a rosy tint, it is much more sober and realistic.

What happens here? During the discovering stage spouses learn to respect the whole personality of their partner. Most of the time they initially fell in love with them because they were so different from themselves. Later on, those differences start to irritate the couple. That is why disillusionment sets in. Now it is time to accept those differences and learn to relate to them positively, valuing them. Each must realize that it is a false goal to try to change the other into their imaginary formula. One partner is different from the other, and that is the best for both. Each must let the other be who he or she is and not force him or her to adjust to the mental dream image. Difference suddenly ceases to be merely a tolerated, necessary evil in the marriage, but a celebrated colorfulness that makes the relationship even richer. Now is the time when a couple realizes that cooperating with the differences gives the marriage new vibrancy. The raw material that will complete each other can now fall into place. They might, for example, discover that one might be a good driver while the other is a great navigator. The driver, then, does not try to stick to his own itinerary at any cost, but lets the other one, who does not prefer the driver's seat, call the shots for the time being. In such cooperation the sense of belonging together strengthens, along with an atmosphere of mutual trust and respect, which leads to a delightful realization: "We are a great team, you and I!"

We do not have to wait until the relationship changes from disillusionment to discovery by itself—we can consciously work toward it. The transition has two important components: learning and relationship building.

Facilitating Discovery by Learning

• ***Commit yourselves to increasing intimacy and to fixing communication!*** During the coldness of disillusionment you have to relearn how to talk to each other, and conversations can open new ways to the deepening of the intimacy. Do not leave it to chance—do it intentionally!

• ***Take part in a good marriage seminar or relationship-building training program to help in transitioning between stages.*** It does not mean that you are doing so badly that you need help! We do not take the car to the mechanic only when something goes wrong—we must also get regular service to confirm that everything is running smoothly and perform routine maintenance.

- ***Help books on marriage or marriage-strengthening movies can stimulate learning.*** Read or watch one together and have a discussion afterward.
- ***If you feel that your holdup in the transition could be an unprocessed childhood trauma, or emotional wounds from a previous relationship, it is worth considering counseling.***
- ***Friends can help strengthen your relationship.*** Get to know other couples who have already lived this stage of a relationship, and learn from them to make the transition easier on your own. It is good to have friends of the same gender at such times, with whom we can talk even more openly about the anxieties or doubts building up inside us.

Helping Discovery Through Relationship-building

As you relearn to live in a marriage, at the same time you can take significant steps toward increasing intimacy even during the process:

- ***Consciously look for positive attributes in your partner that you can help strengthen.*** Your spouse can then regard such confirmations as signs of a progressing relationship.
- ***Encourage each other.***
- ***Listen to each other.***
- ***Support each other's development.*** Help each other in learning, career-building, and the realizing of dreams.
- ***All couples have strengths that they can build on.*** It is always possible to grow, no matter what stage a relationship is in. What does a couple in the discovery stage look like? How do they communicate with each other? For example, how do they have lunch? Ben and Susan are now in this stage, so we will join them to observe how their relationship works. After the previous two stages, it is natural that we visit them at lunch.

Susan (*putting down a plate of toast and scrambled eggs [before setting it down she has to make room, because the table is full of books she needs in order to write an essay]*): Hi, honey, I made you lunch—you know, toast and scrambled eggs. For old times' sake!

Ben (*saying to himself: It's all right that it's scrambled eggs and toast again. I know that Susan is really busy nowadays. She has begun working toward a second degree at the university, and food is not the most important thing. But I'm going to surprise her tomorrow. I'm going to drop the kids off at my parents' and take her to a restaurant for lunch!*): Oh, sweetie, you really shouldn't have to bother with this. I know you are under a lot of pressure, because of the essays. I'm sure I would have found something to eat from the fridge.

After lunch Susan brings up something that she has been thinking about all day.

Susan: I have a surprise for both of us. A new gym has opened in the city, and I have bought a pass for both of us. I've heard that their racquetball court is really good!

Ben: But I thought you didn't like racquetball!

Susan: Well, it's not my favorite game, but I play it to be together with you and to have fun. After that we could go swimming and to the sauna. Are you in?

Such a scene shows that personal interests are now not as important as they were in the disillusionment stage. "We" thinking has formed in the couple, and they have reached an intimate friendship in which they mutually listen to and respect each other.

The common phrases of the discovering stage of marriage:

"I keep finding new things in you from time to time that surprise me."

"What I loved in you the first time . . ."

". . . later on started to annoy me."

"But now I would not change it for anything."

"We are learning to love each other again."

The Deepness Stage

We have seen that after waking from the dream, disillusionment came, with disappointment right behind. However, the situation is not so hopeless that one cannot rediscover his or her partner. When we see the attributes we fell in love with, and learn to value and respect every way in which they differ from us, the relationship grows deeper.

In this phase the couple can finally lean back and enjoy the fruits of everything they have worked so hard to achieve in the previous three stages. The refining of them both has already finished—the cutting burrs, edges, and corners that jutted out from their personalities have worn down, and the two "I"s fit together into a common "we." By this time they have learned to communicate well with each other, and managing their conflicts the right way has become a routine built into their relationship as a basic value. A common harmony reigns between them in their goals, values, and plans. The level of intimacy is high, and nothing threatens the trust between them. The topic of sexuality does not bring pain. Instead, the couple talks with each other openly about their expectations and experiences, and the shadow of emotional blackmail, infidelity, or manipulation no longer exists in their relationship. Is it too good to be true? Does such a thing exist only in fairy tales and movies? No! It is a result of a consciously built-up and lived-out relationship. If the couple has fought their way through the previous three stages and drawn their conclusions and used them, by now they will have arrived at a stress-free love, deeply committed to each other and standing up for each other. And what does such a couple look like? How do they communicate with each other? Let's consider a typical conversation between them before dinner.

Susan and Ben are a freshly retired couple. They enjoy the newly won freedom and are together all the time. It is nearing dinnertime, but Susan was working on her flowers in the garden all afternoon and has not prepared any food.

Ben: You know what, my love? Let's cook something together tonight! It would be so much fun. (*adding with a laugh*) We should learn how to make egg stew! Anyway, I can't eat the toast anymore without my dentures.

Susan: Oh, yes, that will be great! And we should do it more often!

After they have cooked and eaten the dinner spiced with endearment and laughter, Ben continues the conversation:

Ben: Now that I've had my hip replacement surgery I think I am finished with racquetball. We should go to the gardening shop! I have heard that this week they have special discounts for senior citizens. I would like to buy you that special strain of rose you have always wanted.

Susan: Maybe we should go for a walk more often from now on. This way we can get more exercise and have more time to talk with each other.

Of course, we do not actually have to wait until the period of dentures and hip replacements to reach this stage. It's best if we enter this phase when our health lets us enjoy the love with all of its momentum. If we are ready to sacrifice attention, power, and even money for our marriage, it is possible to accelerate the transitions just a bit. Just as in previous occasions, we can draw up the common phrases for this stage as well:

"When I am with you, I feel at home. I am whole."

"If we are separate, I still feel your presence and the safety of our relationship."

"We feel loved."

---

*The dialogue of Susan and Ben was originally presented by Karen and Bernie Holford over the traditional English breakfast of baked beans and toast. It is, thankfully, adapted with their permission.

19

{ mandatory service for married couples }

Earlier in this book I compared marriage preparation to learning how to drive a car. Let me reach back to that metaphor. When we buy a new car from a dealership, it is ready for a person to get in, turn the key, and discover the world with it. It is the same with marriage. After saying "I do," life stretches before you, and you can achieve anything in it that you have dreamed for yourself. But the car does not run without gas, and we have to take it to mandatory service checkups for professional eyes to examine it, change the worn components, and make the necessary adjustments. Our marriage needs feeding and nursing in everyday life too, and sometimes it needs a review. That will reveal what parts are already worn out and which ones we will have to be more careful about. It will require attention and conscious attitude from both of you, because you know that a good marriage is a result of two persons working together. In the following section I will share some thoughts for this mandatory service.

• ***Marriage enrichment seminars.*** Marriage enrichment is not the same as couples' therapy. Therapy usually deals with fixing broken things, while marriage enrichment is for couples who have a good relationship and want to make it even better. Churches and professional organizations frequently offer such programs. They range from weekend or intensive events to weekly sessions. Style, topic choice, effectiveness, and participation fees can vary widely. My friend and colleague Róbert Csizmadia and I have worked out a seminar that processes the building blocks of a happy marriage in ten 90-minute meetings through exercises and games, just as in this book. As a way of examining the effectiveness of the program, we test the participating couples beforehand. Then we repeat the test after the tenth session to find out where they have arrived through the program and again after five or six months to determine what they have managed to apply in their everyday lives. We offer the program as a 10-week event and as a weekend seminar as well. Based on our experience, the two methods have only minimal differences in their effectiveness.

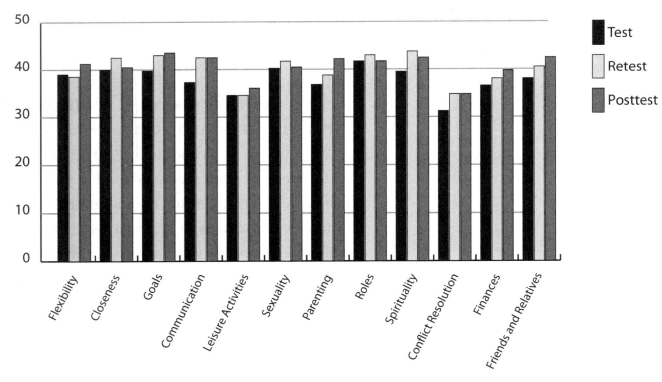

The diagram clearly shows that by the end of the 10 weeks (first and second columns) the participant couples have grown in almost every category. It was what we had expected. However, it was a nice surprise that the growth could be seen even a half year later (third column), and in some categories it even continued beyond that (flexibility, goals, free time, parenting, money, family, and friends). And where the growth did not continue, it still remained higher than at the first testing, so there was no field in which it would revert to the level before the program. Such results convinced us that the quality of marriage can be significantly improved through conscious efforts. International research has also verified that the results of marriage-enrichment seminars can show up even five years after the program.* You will find more details of this program at www.kettenegyutt.hu.

• ***Relationship and family therapy.*** Surely there have been times you could not fix your own car. Such situations can also exist in a relationship as well, when you need the help of a well-prepared professional who can help your relationship and family problems impartially and competently. A therapeutic relationship is always a question of confidence, so it is important to get all the information you can about the person you are going to consult. And during the first meeting, you can ask the therapist more questions before deciding if you want to continue with him or her. Especially consider the following ones: What qualifications make the individual capable of being a counselor or a therapist (most psychologists have a practice in individual therapies; dealing with couples and families needs separate training)? What experience does he or she have in working with couples? Is he or she working alone, or in a therapeutic team with another therapist of the opposite gender, so that the process will equally represent both? To determine their personal sincerity, you can ask about their family status. What relationship evaluation method does he or she use (is an objective evaluation method employed—such as the PREPARE/ENRICH tests—or does their advice come from experience)? How many sessions are needed and how often? How much does a session cost, and when should you pay? Does he or she always want you to come as a couple, or occasionally to meet with you separately? You should decide on therapy only if you have received assuring answers to your questions and if both of you feel confident about the person you will see.

• ***On your own.*** You can do many things at home together without going to any organized programs. If you like to watch DVDs, you can find many on the topic of marriage enrichment. On marriage preparation weekends we like to use the movie *License to Wed* (2007), with Robin Williams. For married couples *The Story of Us* (1999) is also a good one, with Bruce Willis and Michelle Pfeiffer (however, not everyone prefers it, because of the use of some explicit language). Another nice movie, with Jennifer Aniston and Owen Wilson, *Marley & Me* (2008), realistically but optimistically shows—even through the point of view of a dog—the challenges of family life. The best movie I have ever seen on the topic, however, is *Fireproof* (2008), followed next by the success of the Kendrick brothers, *Courageous* (2011). I have successfully used both DVDs in therapeutic situations. All these movies can serve as great conversation starters. Also there are lots of good books that you can read together and discuss. Some authors deliberately craft their books for their audiences to read together, with exercises and conversation topics. Besides DVDs and books, the Couple Checkup is a useful tool for marriage preparation, but it also gives a picture of relationships through different inventories for different life stages of marriage. And if you know your strengths and growth areas, you can intentionally develop the fields of your relationship that need it.

• ***Building friendships.*** Make friends with couples who have also committed themselves to developing their marriage. It can help mutual growth if you have peer couples around you with whom you can talk openly about relationship questions, books, DVDs, and possibly take part in marriage enrichment programs together. No marriage-enrichment foundation, organization, or other association has started without such friendships. The more you talk about the topic, the greater desire you will have to share your findings and experiences with others. Thus it can easily happen that you could become local ambassadors of a good marriage who can help others in living an always-happy marriage.

---

* Howard J. Markman, Mari Jo Renick, Frank J. Floyd, Scott M. Stanley, and Mari Clements, "Preventing Marital Distress Through Communication and Conflict Management Training: A 4- and 5-Year Follow-up," *APA Journal* (2004).

{ appendix: }

Personality Test

Developed by Reinhardt Ruthe, this test will help you discover your personality structure. It was originally published in *Typen und Temperamente: Die vier Persönlichkeitsstrukturen* (Moers: Brendow Verlag, 1999), pp. 148-161. Gábor Mihalec adapted and Robert Csizmadia translated the English version.

Fill out the tests separately. Answer yes or no to each of the 160 statements.

Scoring is based on the yes answers and can be calculated on the pages following the test. A combination of a number and a letter appear after each statement. For example: 97=1B. That means that if you answered yes to statement 97, mark an X in line 97=1B on the scoring sheet.

After completing the scoring sheet, count your total

scores in 1A, 1B, 2A, 2B, 3A, 3B, 4A, and 4B categories, then write them into the final table at the end. This chart contains the description of the personality types and their positive and negative traits. The higher your score in a category, the more characteristic the type for you.

No.	Statement	Yes	No
1.	I like to work on my own, taking responsibility for myself.		
2.	I'm a withdrawing person.		
3.	I'm straightforward and possibly undiplomatic in my relationships.		
4.	I tell my critique even to those I love.		
5.	If it's necessary I can be a good leader, but it is difficult for me to understand the problems of my colleagues and employees.		
6.	I have a tendency to be obstinate.		
7.	I don't enjoy working with children.		
8.	It seems that no one can understand me.		
9.	I'm in a constant rush, because I do several things at a time.		
10.	Sometimes I find myself planning the next working hours and tasks during a meal.		
11.	I like jumping from one idea to the next when a new one comes to mind.		
12.	I can imagine a long-term relationship without marriage.		
13.	Everybody should keep his or her independence in friendship and marriage.		
14.	I'm reserved at first in new relationships.		
15.	I can enjoy fine and beautiful things alone as well as with others.		
16.	I try to process the loss alone when an important relationship breaks down.		
17.	I prefer to keep unpleasant things to myself rather than speak about them.		
18.	I pull myself together and try to resolve problems myself instead of looking for help.		
19.	I'm satisfied in a sexual relationship if my partner does not need too much closeness and affection.		
20.	Sometimes I like to spend time away from home to escape family confusion.		
21.	I'm not particularly worried if my relatives or neighbors are at odds with the law.		
22.	I keep worrying about my looks and wonder what other people think of me.		
23.	Because I need recognition and confirmation, I'm very sensitive to criticism.		
24.	In my dealings with others I emphasize generosity and tolerance.		

No.	Statement	Yes	No
25.	I can conceal problems and bad moods well.		
26.	I have no difficulty taking risks.		
27.	If it has to be, I can entertain a large group.		
28.	I am an important personality.		
29.	Instead of working out a problem with others, I would prefer solving it in my own mind.		
30.	At times I feel that everybody conspires against me.		
31.	Sometimes I do not recognize friends and acquaintances on the street if they don't wave at me.		
32.	I can easily give a cold shoulder, just to show how independent I am.		
33.	I could distance myself from family rules and customs and live my own way.		
34.	When I'm convinced of an idea, I push it through.		
35.	I often take on things that others might not consider to be my personal responsibility.		
36.	Compared to others, I can easily enter dangerous situations.		
37.	I am more nervous than others.		
38.	I find it difficult to bond deeply with others.		
39.	My mother was loving and caring.		
40.	I like dealing with children, since I am family-oriented.		
41.	In conversation with others, I don't like to be the only one holding my viewpoint.		
42.	I enjoy getting to know people during my holiday trips.		
43.	I'm very gentle when I criticize those I love.		
44.	If possible, I try to avoid illness, poverty, or suffering.		
45.	I find it difficult to trust and rely on others.		
46.	I have many thoughts and fantasies, but I do not share them with others.		
47.	I think about the meaning of life, but I never talk about it with others.		
48.	If possible, I try to plan my life, my household, and my work carefully.		
49.	I do not leave much freedom for myself or for others.		
50.	I have a tendency toward intolerance and strict judgment.		
51.	I take it very hard if someone points out my mistakes.		
52.	Others think I'm opinionated or a know-it-all, but I feel I only pay attention to what is right.		
53.	Many times I feel like a slave to duty.		
54.	I'm generally interested in what those around me think of me.		

No.	Statement	Yes	No
55.	It is often difficult for me to trust my own judgment without the affirmation of others.		
56.	It is very difficult for me to be alone, because I like to do things with others.		
57.	I greatly desire to be a benefit to others.		
58.	I have difficulty sleeping, and when I'm awake I often brood over things.		
59.	I envy the good fortune of others.		
60.	I have less confidence compared to others.		
61.	Attack and criticism can really hurt me.		
62.	Sometimes I feel really useless.		
63.	I like participating in joint activities with my friends and my partner.		
64.	I love sharing new and beautiful things with others.		
65.	I want to comfort those struggling with sickness, suffering, or death.		
66.	I like to experience the new and unknown.		
67.	I'm excited to experience new adventures.		
68.	If I don't like a television program, I just surf on and look for something else.		
69.	I prefer to dress in fashionable colors, vibrant style, and in contemporary trends.		
70.	My basic nature is one of optimism and zest for life.		
71.	When it comes to money, I am especially generous.		
72.	If I tell about an experience, I tend to dramatize it.		
73.	I can be enthusiastic about a lot of simple matters.		
74.	Hyperactivity and busyness characterize my life.		
75.	It is important for me to collect and preserve. I have a hard time throwing anything away.		
76.	Absolute reliability is an important priority, in my opinion.		
77.	I do not let life overwhelm me. I like to keep things under my own control.		
78.	I never find enough closeness in a relationship.		
79.	I wish I could do everything together with my partner.		
80.	I will even criticize and attack someone to ensure closeness and care.		
81.	I easily realize the needs and wishes of those close to me.		
82.	Some days I have no energy and would prefer not to get out of bed.		
83.	I find it difficult to focus my thoughts on a particular task.		
84.	I sometimes find it hard to motivate myself.		

No.	Statement	Yes	No
85.	I can be cold to others so that they will realize the seriousness of what they did to me and will then treat me better.		
86.	I usually need someone to assist me both with minor and major decisions.		
87.	If I'm alone, I feel helpless. I will do everything I can to prevent loneliness.		
88.	My mood swings sometimes range from despair to euphoria.		
89.	I have constipation for long periods.		
90.	I find it difficult to guess the wishes and needs of people close to me.		
91.	I find it difficult to trust others, because I do not understand them.		
92.	I treat people with caution and suspicion.		
93.	I find it difficult to concentrate on my work.		
94.	I prefer dealing with things rather than people.		
95.	I mostly resolve problems and difficulties alone.		
96.	I am rather unemotional and indifferent.		
97.	It is easy for me to withdraw from the presence of others.		
98.	When I was a child, I felt that my mother was restrictive and oppressive.		
99.	Whatever I start, I persist at it.		
100.	Conscientiousness, punctuality, and good time management are my strengths.		
101.	My dress code is generally moderate, conservative, and inconspicuous.		
102.	In my work I need clearly defined guidelines and boundaries.		
103.	I am convinced that tasks must be carried out perfectly.		
104.	I like it when everything is clear and unambiguous.		
105.	I am able to exert great effort to achieve my goals.		
106.	Rules and clear guidelines make my life easier.		
107.	I want to do the right thing, and I have high moral standards.		
108.	I do not like to draw attention to myself, so I avoid having to speak in front of large groups.		
109.	People say they can tell where they stand with me.		
110.	I carefully consider tasks before I attend to them, even if they are only minor ones.		
111.	I do not take risks without careful consideration beforehand.		
112.	I like to work under a boss who assumes ultimate responsibility. I'd rather tend to the details.		
113.	I would never submit my resignation because of a sudden impulse. I plan everything in advance.		
114.	In matters of conscience I rely on my head, not on my heart.		

No.	Statement	Yes	No
115.	I desire an intimate and long-lasting bond with another person.		
116.	Understanding, connection, and exchange of ideas are needed in case of problems and difficulties.		
117.	I need closeness and care from others.		
118.	Farewell situations are always hard on me.		
119.	My self-control and conscience often get me into stressful situations.		
120.	I'm not funny or flexible.		
121.	I value consistency. Too much flexibility is weakness in my eyes.		
122.	People consider me a tyrant at home, at work, and at church, because I pinpoint their flaws.		
123.	I show a good mood even when I'm sad inside.		
124.	It is difficult to commit myself.		
125.	I can easily repress unpleasant things.		
126.	I love diversity in friendship and in love as well.		
127.	I strive for the best results in many areas. If I fail to achieve this, I'm unhappy.		
128.	Since I have high moral standards, it is difficult for me to talk about things that I find wrong.		
129.	I have confidence.		
130.	I can efficiently sell my goals, ideas, and projects.		
131.	I like sports in which seemingly infinite space and distance play an important role (e.g., cross-country skiing, flying, diving).		
132.	As a Christian, I feel my faith is childlike.		
133.	For me, things are either good or bad. I cannot stand cowardly opportunism.		
134.	I often struggle with doubt, wondering if I made the right decision.		
135.	I feel useless and helpless when others do not take my ideas seriously, especially if they question or ridicule them.		
136.	In certain areas (faith, work, child-rearing) I am inclined to fanaticism.		
137.	I find it difficult to be open to new things.		
138.	I like to champion principles.		
139.	I find it hard to forgive myself if I make a mistake in my work or in my life.		
140.	If things get out of control, I lose my confidence.		
141.	I tend to be impatient if I see that the other party does not accept my ideas.		
142.	I need rituals to ease my life.		

No.	Statement	Yes	No
143.	I withhold my emotions in all human relations.		
144.	I'm not a social person, but I am creative in many areas.		
145.	I am primarily an observer and not swayed by emotion.		
146.	I can free myself totally from the need for recognition and am not bothered by criticism.		
147.	I try to put myself at the center of attention in any kind of gathering.		
148.	I can easily impress my audience.		
149.	I cannot get enough appreciation and admiration.		
150.	My desire for freedom is almost limitless.		
151.	Sometimes I feel a strong urge to do something provocative.		
152.	I do not mind if someone sits down at my table at a restaurant.		
153.	I want to talk about my problems and difficulties to people I trust.		
154.	I enjoy working with others or in a team, because then I have backing.		
155.	I'm sexually satisfied if I get closeness, mutuality, and tenderness.		
156.	I love surprises, and I am always open to new ideas.		
157.	I want everyone to like me, not only my friends.		
158.	I felt my mother was a person who provided me with freedom and attention, and admired my ideas.		
159.	My slogan is: "Generosity even in the smallest of things."		
160.	Sometimes I need to leave home to experience new things and to escape daily routine.		

Scoring			
1=1A	41=2A	81=2B	121=3B
2=1A	42=2A	82=2B	122=3B
3=1A	43=2A	83=2B	123=4B
4=1A	44=1B	84=2B	124=4B
5=1B	45=1B	85=2B	125=4B
6=1B	46=1B	86=2B	126=4B
7=1B	47=1B	87=2B	127=3B
8=1B	48=3A	88=2B	128=3B
9=4B	49=3A	89=2B	129=4A
10=4B	50=3B	90=1B	130=4A
11=4B	51=3B	91=1B	131=4A
12=4B	52=3B	92=1B	132=4A
13=1A	53=3B	93=1B	133=3B
14=1A	54=2A	94=1B	134=3B
15=1A	55=2A	95=1A	135=3B
16=1A	56=2A	96=1A	136=3B
17=1A	57=2A	97=1B	137=3B
18=1A	58=2B	98=1B	138=3B
19=1A	59=2B	99=3A	139=3B
20=1A	60=2B	100=3A	140=3B
21=4B	61=2B	101=3A	141=3B
22=4B	62=2B	102=3A	142=3B
23=4B	63=2A	103=3A	143=1A
24=4A	64=2A	104=3A	144=1A
25=4A	65=2A	105=4A	145=1A
26=4A	66=4A	106=3A	146=1A
27=4A	67=4A	107=3A	147=4B
28=4A	68=4A	108=3A	148=4B
29=1B	69=4A	109=3A	149=4B
30=1B	70=4A	110=3A	150=4B
31=1B	71=4B	111=3A	151=4B
32=1B	72=4B	112=3A	152=2A
33=1A	73=4B	113=3A	153=2A
34=1A	74=4B	114=3A	154=2A
35=2B	75=3A	115=2A	155=2A
36=2B	76=3A	116=2A	156=4A
37=2B	77=3A	117=2A	157=4A
38=1B	78=2B	118=2A	158=4A
39=2A	79=2B	119=3B	159=4A
40=2A	80=2B	120=3B	160=4A

	Summary			
	1A	1B	2A	2B
	schizoid personality (rather positive)	schizoid personality (rather negative)	depressed personality (rather positive)	depressed personality (rather negative)
Total Points:				
Total:				
	3A	3B	4A	4B
	obsessive personality (rather positive)	obsessive personality (rather negative)	hysterical personality (rather positive)	hysterical personality (rather negative)
Total Points:				
Total:				

schizoid personality scores:	
depressed personality scores:	
obsessive personality scores:	
hysterical personality scores:	

{appendix}

Notes

Notes

Notes

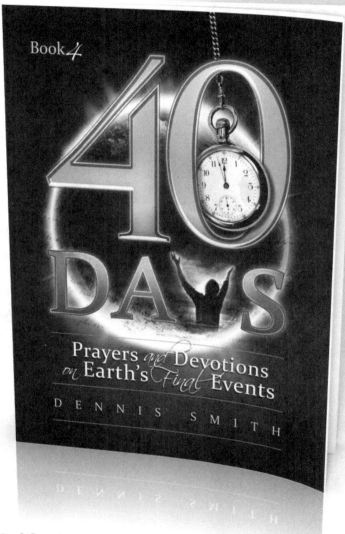

This Could *Change* Everything

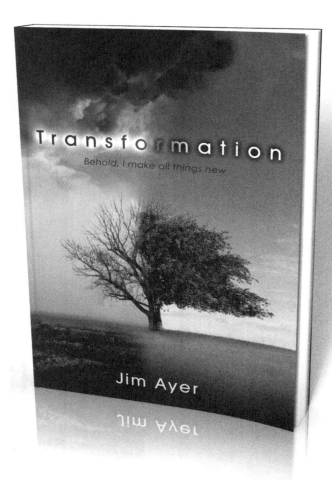

Find transforming power for your life

Your Daily Journey to Transformation
A 12-week Study Guide
Paperback
978-0-8280-2702-1

Remodeling Your Life DVD
God's Transforming Power
Jim Ayer's TV series on DVD.
Twelve 30-minute episodes.
3-DVD set.
978-0-8280-2746-5

Do you feel like temptations always beat you into submission? You can't seem to win a victory and wonder if you're not trying hard enough, or if God isn't holding up His end of the bargain.

In the book, *Transformation*, Jim Ayer opens up about his own experience as a serial sinner and tells how he connected with the power that God has provided to change us from the inside out.

A companion study guide, *Your Daily Journey to Transformation*, Jim and Janene Ayer take individuals or small groups on a 12-week journey toward a transformed life— a life shaped and energized by the Holy Spirit.

"Behold, I make all things new," says Jesus. See that promise fulfilled in your life today. Paperback, 978-0-8280-2711-3

Availability subject to change.

AdventistBookCenter.com | 800.765.6955

Review&Herald®
Spread the Word